Gats, Gams, and Guts

A Field Guide to the Dark World of Film Noir

By Pierre V. Comtois

"Gats, Gams, and Guts: A Field Guide to the Dark World of Film Noir," by Pierre V. Comtois. ISBN 978-1-63868-028-4 (softcover).

Published 2021 by Virtualbookworm.com Publishing Inc., P.O. Box 9949, College Station, TX 77842, US.

Contents

3

Introduction

I first discovered film noir on an unconscious level. That is, when I watched all those murder mysteries and crime movies when I was a kid on the flickering screen or our family's black and white TV, I didn't understand what I was looking at. Oh, sure, I knew the private dick was sleuthing away to find the murderer, or the criminal gang was scheming to rob the armored car, or the poor sap was being drawn into a situation that could only mean bad things for him, but what I didn't realize was that they were all part of a single genre with similarities in theme, character, location, and cinematography that could be identified, tabulated, and defined. A process that had begun with French film critic Nino Frank way back in 1946. (Well before my time!)

At a time when these kind of films were referred to simply as melodramas, Frank saw a pattern that included post-war cynicism that manifested itself by way of physical representation utilizing black and white photography and lighting and location shooting. It also included an uncompromising depiction of mean streets and back alleys through a cold, unfeeling camera lens. The combination, as Frank put it, could be described as *film noir,* French for black or dark cinema. And many of these films could be pretty dark, mainly those that featured normal, innocent people making a single wrong decision (usually breaking the law in some way or falling for the wiles of a scheming femme fatale [another phrase we have the French to thank for!]) and a plot that relentlessly pursues the consequences of that action to its bitter conclusion. The best films with this kind of plot are those that end with the formerly innocent protagonist either being ruined or killed.

Other kinds of noir would cover subjects from the crook's point of view, their planning and execution of a heist, perhaps their falling out, and then their pursuit by the law. Others might be the docudrama, the love gone bad, police procedural, or even psychological breakdown.

Of course, the classic format of film noir was the earliest to be established, namely that of the private eye doggedly working a case while avoiding run ins with both criminals and the cops. This earliest incarnation of film noir was kicked off by the *Maltese Falcon* (not the 1931 version but the 1941 version). Adapted from the novel by Dashiell Hammett, it follows private eye Sam Spade as he makes his way among suspicious gumshoes, scheming criminals, and lying women to find the statuette of the title. These earliest noirs were often adapted from or inspired by crime stories that had become popular in such pulp magazines of the 1930s as *Black Mask Detective* or *True Crime* where authors such as Hammett, Raymond Chandler, and James M. Cain plied their trade. In fact, Chandler had once credited fellow writer Hammett for taking murder out of the drawing room and putting it into the gutter where it belonged. Just so. And Hollywood followed.

It was director John Huston who decided to remake *The Maltese Falcon* but his version would stick closer to the source material resulting in a taut, cold blooded depiction of a criminal underworld peopled by cynical private eyes and world weary cops. It set a pattern. *The Big Sleep* starred PI Philip Marlowe who ends up getting drugged and beaten up along the way to solving the murder. Marlowe is also featured in *The Lady in the Lake* where he again has no easy time getting to the bottom of things.

Still, though Hollywood took much of its inspiration from the pulps, it had made crime films even earlier that featured some elements of film noir if not its particular ambiance. Those were the first films I encountered as a youngster. Films like *The Roaring Twenties* where James Cagney often starred but who'd be largely absent from crime films as the 1940s and 50s moved on.

By the time I was a teenager and well on my way to becoming a film buff proper, Humphrey Bogart had reemerged in the pop culture of the mid to late 1960s as the epitome of cool. With his rumpled trench coat, fedora with brim turned down casting shadows over his face, and cigarette dangling from his lips, he was a favorite poster subject for bedroom walls. His interpretation of Spade and Marlowe as tough, cynical, world weary dicks with their own strict moral codes became the embodiment of the American type. While John Wayne, another Hollywood icon who remained popular in those years (along with W.C. Fields!), captured the pioneer spirit of another age, Bogart was that of the modern city dweller threatened no longer by Indians but criminals who dwelt in the shadows and back alleys of the big city.

The early 1940s crime films of Bogart and Robert Mitchum and Robert Montgomery were what I refer to as proto-noirs. Often filmed on sets rather than actual locations and featuring big name stars in well financed A pictures put out by major studios, they were a little too mannered to be the genuine article but they made for a solid bridge from early crime pictures to legit film noirs. That said, it was likely Bogart who led me into the deep end of the noir pool as my determination to watch any and all black and white movies increased. And many of those films, caught late at night, on often snowy TV channels, were noirs populated by the likes of Robert Ryan, Dana Andrews, Alan Ladd, Robert Ryan,and Fred MacMurray. And then there were the women. Whether femme fatales or la meilleur femme (as I came to call those women who inspired the male protagonist to be his best rather than seducing him into doing his worst) film noir was populated by some of the most attractive ladies on the Hollywood lists including Lizbeth Scott, Audrey Totter, Faith Domergue, Barbara Stanwyck, and Ann Savage. I came to know and love them all as you will too as you begin your own journey into the world of noir.

But before you do, a few words on the book you hold in your hands. Undoubtedly, you will discover your own favored stars and vehicles as you explore the genre. The entries that follow are meant only as a guide of what I consider the best or the most notorious noirs with a sprinkling of those films to avoid if you can. Furthermore, the entries here by no means exhaust the list of films that can be categorized as noirs. There were literally hundreds of such films made. So the following entries must be considered a list of the better known...and a starting point from which the interested fan can seek out the gems that even I have yet to discover!

The Roaring Twenties (1939)

While too soon in film history to be considered even a proto-noir on the level of *The Maltese Falcon* or *The Big Sleep, The Roaring Twenties* does include the basic noir formula of an ordinary Joe making that single wrong turn that proves fatal. The film tells the tale of the epic rise and fall of a generic mob leader during the years when prohibition was the law of the land. Eddie Bartlett (played by James Cagney) is a soldier returning from the killing fields of World War I Europe only to find that not only is his service barely recognized but that the country he left has changed with paying jobs at a minimum. Forced into working as a part time cab driver, he inadvertantly becomes involved in the underworld of illicit liquor sales. After being pinched for the possession of alcohol, Eddie makes that one wrong move: he decides to get in on the ground floor of what promises to be an unlawful but lucrative business. Before you know it, Eddie is brewing his own bathtub booze and developing his own network of customers. The money begins to flow and he invests in a fleet of taxi cabs, triumphs over rival gangs, and joins forces with fellow veteran George Hally (Humphrey Bogart), now in the smuggling trade. But at the height of Eddie's success, the stock market crashes and he loses everything, including Jean Sherman (Priscilla Lane) the girl he'd set his sights on. Busted all the way back to driving a cab, he becomes an alcoholic and, in a final act of redemption, ends up confronting and killing Hally. In the process, he too is shot, stumbles from Hally's townhouse, and manages to reach the steps of a nearby church before falling dead. That's where boozy songbird (Gladys George) ends up cradling him in her arms. When asked by an investigating copper who the man in her arms is, she provides the movie's most famous line: "He used to be a big shot!" Straightforward direction by Hal B. Wallis and a tight script by Jerry Wald (based on the experiences of columnist Mark Hellinger) keep the story moving forward at a relentlessly entertaining pace with no little help from Cagney whose magnetic personality carries the film all the way to its crash landing of an ending. In broadest possible terms, the film anticipates the major trope of later film noir: a man who yields to temptation and pays the price.

Bootlegger James Cagney (Eddie Bartlett) strikes up a partnership with smuggler George Hally (Humphrey Bogart)

End of the line: Eddie Bartlett (James Cagney) gets the drop on former partner George Hally (Humphrey Bogart) at the climax to *The Roaring Twenties*

Forbidden fruit: Pretty Priscilla Lane as ingenue Jean Sherman was plainly too young for WWI vet Eddie Bartlett but in true noir tradition, his obsession with her led to his downfall.

The Maltese Falcon (1941)

It was the film that kicked off the genre, the ne plus ultra of film noir! Adapted from the novel by Dashiell Hammett, the dean of hard boiled detective fiction writers of the *Black Mask* school, *The Maltese Falcon* has it all: atmosphere, mystery, murder, twists, turns, sharp dialogue, complexity, and sex...well the off screen kind that is nonetheless implied in no uncertain terms. That said, the romantic sub-plot between Sam Spade (played by Humphrey Bogart in his breakout role) and Brigid O'Shaughnessy (Mary Astor) is the only thing that doesn't really work in this otherwise perfect film. It's just not developed enough to be convincing. There just wasn't enough time and too much else going on in the story for director/screenwriter John Huston to concentrate on! A story that focused on a legendary and priceless avian statue called the Maltese Falcon ("The stuff dreams are made of") and the ring of ruthless conspirators who'd do anything to get their hands on it including "Fat man" Kaspar Gutman (Sydney Greenstreet); Joel Cairo (Peter Lorre); and O'Shaughnessy herself. Hangers on also included the never seen Floyd Thursby and the blink or you'll miss him Captain Jacoby (played by Huston's father, an uncredited Walter Huston). Along the way there's murder: Thursby and Jacoby are killed by loose trigger fingered Wilmer Cook (Eisha Cook, Jr) and Spade's partner Miles Archer is murdered by O'Shaughnessy. In the novel, Spade is a randy sort being involved with his partner's wife before falling into bed with the dangerous O'Shaughnessy. Spade even strip searches O'Shaughnessy for money Gutman claimed she stole, a scene that was left out of the movie for obvious reasons! Those elements, as well as Cairo's homosexuality, are only hinted at in the film. But it's just as well, as they'd only cheapen the characters and distract from the exciting plot as the bird falls into Spade's possession putting him in the catbird seat so to speak vis a vis the conspirators. Everything about the film sets the tone for all the film noirs to follow: moody cinematography by Arthur Edeson; the cynical hero/detective; the femme fatale; the nighted sets (although actual location shooting would become a hallmark of noir, here, the action is limited to studio soundstages and backlots); flawed personalities and a focus on criminal activity; murder and mystery. Huston's direction is flawless and untangles the film's convoluted plot with clockwork precision. (It helped director and cast keep all the details straight by having shot the picture in proper sequence) Casting is near perfect (except for Astor who just isn't alluring enough to make it believable that Spade would bother with her over Lee Patrick's obviously adoring secretary) with Bogart becoming an instant icon with his world weary features, smoking cigarette, fedora, and trench coat (the look would become cool all over again in the late 1960s when classic films enjoyed a revival in local movie houses). Altogether, *The Maltese Falcon* is a must see for any fans of noir or any movie fans at all!

Marlowe's partner, Miles Archer listens in on Brigid O'Shaunnesey's sob story (dba Ruth Wonderly) before falling for it...to his regret!

Humphrey Bogart as Philip Marlowe, Peter Lorre as Joel Cairo, Mary Astor as Brigid O'Shaunessy, and Sidney Greenstreet as Kaspar Gutman sharpen their knives over the black bird

Iconic portrait of Humphrey Bogart as Philip Marlowe, Sam Spade, or Rick Blaine, take your pick! With posters like this hanging on bedroom walls across America, Bogart redefined what it meant to be cool in the late 1960s

The Glass Key (1942)

The Glass Key falls into that group of forties films produced just prior to the advent of proper film noir that emerged in the post-war era. It's also of those films (often based on hard boiled pulp stories and novels that originally gave birth to the noir attitude) that bridge the gap between straight crime films of the thirties and noir proper. As with classic pulp novelists such as Dashiell Hammett, Raymond Chandler, and James M. Cain, films such as *The Glass Key* usually involved police and political corruption, the lure of the underworld for the unwary, wrong choices made, and forces at work beyond the control of the protagonist. Such are the many ingredients that make up this film as corrupt ward heeler Paul Madvig (played by Brian Donlevy) decides to turn a new leaf by cleaning up the town. His motivation is love for the daughter of gubernatorial candidate Ralph Henry (Moroni Olsen) the beautiful and sultry Janet Henry (Veronica Lake). But when Henry's ne'er do well son Taylor (Richard Denning) shows up dead, Madvig is primed to take the fall. His situation isn't helped when his kid sister, Opal (Bonita Granville) turns state's evidence out of the belief that her brother killed Taylor, whom she was seeing against his wishes. Enter Madvig right hand man, Ed Beaumont (Alan Ladd) who sets out to prove his boss didn't do the deed. But the odds are against him and through the course of the film, is not only stymied by Madvig himself, but becomes the victim of a brutal beating by Jeff (William Bendix), a bruiser in the employ of gangster Nick Varna (Joseph Calleia). Finally, through a combination of sleuthing and slight of hand, Ed wins out: he saves Madvig from the electric chair and scoops Janet for himself. *The Glass Key*, adapted from the novel by Dashiell Hammett, is one of a handful of proto-noir, Hollywood A films that ooze darkness and shadows and a cast of characters none of whom can be trusted. Director Stuart Heisler does a good job keeping things moving forward so that there isn't a single slow scene while cinematographer Theodor Sparkuhl makes his contribution to the look of the genre. But the cast is what really makes this film hum including peekaboo girl Veronica Lake, she of the enigmatic smile and up and comer Alan Ladd who seemingly doesn't know *how* to smile. William Bendix is unforgettable as the brutal Jeff who enjoys pulling the wings off flies or gleefully beating prisoners like Beaumont to an inch of his life. Richard Denning has a small role but he makes the most of it and Bonita Granville, who made her mark in a series of earlier Nancy Drew mysteries, is all grown up now and suitably vulnerable. And could we forget Brian Donlevy who chews the scenery every chance he gets? No way! This film has it all and it's incredibly entertaining, keeping viewers guessing while emersing them in its noir world of hoods, gangsters, corrupt pols, and scheming babes. Not to be missed!

All in a day's work: Alan Ladd's Ed Beaumont collapses after getting the business from the brutish Jeff played by William Bendix

As ward heeler Paul Madvig's fixer, Alan Ladd's Ed Beaumont prepares to do Brian Donlevy's dirty work including breaking up his sister's latest liason

Nancy Drew grows up: It's plain here why Bonita Granville was able to leap quickly from juvenile to adult roles!

This Gun For Hire (1942)

A proto-noir, this film follows loner Philip Raven (played by Alan Ladd in his debut role) a former abused child who now takes his rage out at the world as a hired killer. Interestingly, though Ladd isn't top billed, it's his stone cold portrayal of the largely emotionless Raven that steals the show. Not that eye candy Veronica Lake is chopped liver! The mystique that made her a star is clearly on display here as she sings and wisecracks here way across the screen. Boyfriend Det. Michael Crane (Robert Preston) by comparison comes across as too bland for someone like Lake's vivacious Ellen Graham. (Who's employed by the Neptune Club as a slinky songstress who also performs magic tricks!) The intense Ladd would seem the more suited of the two except for the fact that he's already killed two people (including a woman) for the traitorous Willard Gates (Laird Cregar). In fact, the first scene in the movie has him slapping around a cleaning woman for shooing a kitten out of his cheap room. He and Ellen meet on a train after he tries to steal a fin from her purse. Not a nice guy. Ellen herself, has been recruited by the government to worm her way into the affections of Gates in order to get the goods on his employer who's suspected of making a deal with unnamed foreign powers to sell them a new kind of poison gas. She and Raven come together after Gates pays Raven off with stolen bills. Raven is out to kill Gates for double crossing him. The script, by Albert Maltz and W.R. Burnett is based on a novel by Graham Green with direction by one Frank Tuttle. Cinematography is by John Seltz who excels when the action moves to a local oil refinery and thence to a nearby train yard. The espionage plot can get hokey at times but Ladd and Lake have the star power to bring it off and even if they didn't, who cares? While not strictly film noir in the classic sense, *This Gun For Hire* nevertheless includes elements necessary for laying the groundwork for the true noir films to follow.

Ellen Graham (Veronica Lake) opens *This Gun For Hire* with a bit of whimsy as she adds song and magic to her other more obvious charms!

Not a nice guy: cold blooded hit man Philip Raven (Alan Ladd) prepares to slap around the cleaning lady for mistreating a stray cat

Over the years, Graham Greene would find many of his novels adapted to the screen including *The Quiet American, The Third Man,* and *A Gun For Sale* (as *This Gun For Hire*)

The Woman in the Window (1944)

This film noir has it both ways: the ending where the hapless protagonist hits rock bottom and the happy ending. It's not a formula that one would expect to work but in this case it kind of does providing the film with not one but two twist endings! Edward G. Robinson plays middle aged family man Prof. Richard Wanley who falls in with beautiful and mysterious Alice Reed (Joan Bennett), the subject of a portrait on display in a big picture window. As Wanley examines the picture, lo and behold, its subject appears and after some come hither talk, he's lured to the woman's apartment. While there, one of Reed's johns shows up and in a jealous rage, attacks Wanley. Reed presses a pair of scissors into Wanley's hand and voila! His attacker is killed in self defense. But aware that his presence in Reed's apartment would be a scandal he couldn't live down, Wanley suggests getting rid of the body and leaving the police out of it. There are more wrinkles after this turning point decision including a blackmailing Dan Duryea (Heidt) and DA Frank Lalor (Raymond Massey), a friend of Wanley's whose investigation of the case makes for some uncomfortable moments for the professor. Suffice it to say, when things go south, and a plot to murder Heidt falls through, Wanley commits suicide. But surprise! Heidt is gunned down by police before he can talk and Reed's phone call to Wanley comes too late to save him! But where Reed couldn't help, the production code could. Director Fritz Lang was told that he couldn't end the film with a suicide and solved the problem by simply tacking on an ending wherein we discover that Wanley had dreamed up the whole thing! Instead of ruining the ending, the double whammy only adds to this film's interest. Lang does a good job building the suspense and cinematographer Milton Krasner rises to the occasion despite all the scenes being shot on a soundstage and on backlots. Robinson is suitably milquetoast while Bennett manages to convey a combination of sultry allure and suggested evil without actually coming right out and confirming it. Was she bad or wasn't she? She made it hard to tell. Good stuff. So much so that it led to a reuniting of Lang and the Robinson, Bennett, and Duryea team in the next year's *Scarlet Street*. **Fun fact:** Don't blink or you'll miss the appearances of two ex-Little Rascals: Robert Blake and Spanky McFarland!

Slinky Joan Bennett, noir femme fatale deluxe!

14

Joan Bennett as Alice Reed gets set to slip blackmailer Dan Duryea's Heidt a mickey

The bars on the fence foreshadow Prof Wanley's fate should the murder he committed and then covered up be discovered

Murder, My Sweet (1944)

Excellent early proto-film noir in the manner of *Maltese Falcon/Big Sleep*. That's because it was an adaptation of *Black Mask Detective* alumnus Raymond Chandler's novel, *Farewell My Lovely*, a convoluted mystery about stolen jewels, missing lounge singers, and, oh, yeah, murder! The main character is private eye Philip Marlowe (played by former ingenue Dick Powell with suitable cynicism) who tells the tale first person allowing for his acerbic comments and snide asides that made reading hard boiled fiction such a delight. The film, directed by Edward Dmytryk, opens with a scene of Marlowe under police grilling, his eyes bandaged. From there, he tells how he came to be blinded beginning with a visit in his office by burly bruiser Moose Malloy (Mike Mazurki) who hires him to find missing girlfriend Velma Valento. From there, Marlowe finds himself embroiled in a hot jewelry ring involving upper crust psychiatrist Jules Amthor (Otto Kruger) who blackmails his rich clients after they spill their guts to him while under analysis. In between all that are a pair of femme fatales including Ann Grayle (Anne Shirley), pretty, protective, daughter to rich Leuwen Grayle (Miles Mander) and Leuwen's young wife, the dangerous Helen (Clair Trevor). Which one will be Marlowe's downfall? Ah, that would be telling! Suffice it to say that *Murder, My Sweet* is a solid adaptation of the novel by scriptwriter John Paxton (despite some changes due to the production code) and cinematography by Harry Wild, particularly in scenes at the beach house where everything is revealed, the private hospital where Marlowe is drugged and held prisoner, and in Marlowe's office where a cool effect is had when the words on the office window are cast onto the figure of Amthor henchman, Lindsey Marriot as he sits before Marlowe's desk. A great hard boiled, mystery noir that Hollywood produced routinely in the 1940s and failed to replicate again in the years following the 1950s. (The coming of color destroyed this kind of filmmaking)

Careful Marlowe! Danger ahead!

Anne Shirley (nee Evelyn Paris, Dawn O'Day) grew up fast from her portrayal of L.M. Montgomery's pre-teen heroine Anne of Green Gables to Anne Grayle in *Murder, My Sweet*!

Marlowe suspects he's been had...seconds before he's run off the road!

Double Indemnity (1944)

Possibly the best depiction of the classic film noir formula of average guy making the wrong decision and ruining his life because of it. That's exactly what happens to insurance agent Walter Neff (played by noir pace setter Fred MacMurray) here as, made stupid with sex (although to be sure, it is only suggested in the film), he decides to conspire with slinky Phyllis Dietrichson (Barbara Stanwyck in a blond wig and ankle bracelet) to kill her unappreciative husband, collect his $100,000 in insurance money, and live happily ever after. It was a pipe dream but one Walter allows himself to believe overcome as he is with desire for Phyllis. But Phyllis has more up her bath towel than satisfying Walter's desires. She's actually cheating on him with her daughter's boyfriend and has already murdered her husband's first wife. She's been playing Walter for a sucker, something he realizes far too late. The film was an adaptation of the novel by James M. Cain (based on an actual event), one that was considered impossible to make under the Hayes Code but screenwriter's Billy Wilder and Raymond Chandler manage to do it substituting leading dialogue and double entendres for literal sex scenes. Walter's first meeting with Phyllis for instance is a graduate class in how to write suggestive dialogue as the two spar with Phyllis ending up by telling Walter he's doing 90 miles per hour in a slow lane. Walter's fascination with Phyllis' ankle bracelet is symbolic for a lust he can barely control. And when Phyllis shows up at his apartment with eager lips and tight sweater...well! Directed by Wilder, the movie moves along like a freight train headed for a collision as Walter narrates in hard boiled style telling the story of his fall for Phyllis and their conspiracy to kill her husband. Tension mounts as Walter brings claims adjuster Barton Keyes (Edward G. Robinson) into the narrative whose mounting suspicions provide the suspense. Los Angeles locations and cinematography by John Seitz provide the somber atmosphere for a film that takes place almost completely after dark, where lights are constantly being turned on and off in midnight apartments, and characters sit in shadowed offices listening to or whispering into dictaphone machines. No more words can adequately describe how great this film is. You just have to see it to believe it!

Exceeding the speed limit: Phyllis Dietrichson (Barbara Stanwyck) seduces Walter Neff (Fred MacMurray) with a deadly combination of hungry lips, a tight sweater, and an ankle bracelet

You know it's a noir when the venetian blinds cast shadows over everything! Walter Neff tells all into his dictaphone, kicking off the story in flashback

A close shave: Neff's boss Barton Keyes (Edward G. Robinson) throws a scare into the scheming couple when he drops by to talk over his latest theories

Phantom Lady (1944)

Phantom Lady falls into that mid-range category of noir films (between crime and true noir) inspired by the pulp fiction of Dashiell Hammett and Raymond Chandler in that it's built around a murder mystery that needs to be solved by the picture's end. Coupled with incredible black and white cinematography by Woody Bredell, it becomes a solid entry in the genre albeit taken down a peg by Carol Richman (Ella Raines) who plays her part with a whiff of Nancy Drew (punctuated by her hysterical screaming near the end: "You're mad, mad, mad!") But these minor criticisms pale in comparison to the film's rich photography and intriguing plot. The key element to that plot being a funny hat worn by the titular "phantom lady" with whom engineer Scott Henderson (Alan Curtis) takes up following a row with his wife. Returning home, Henderson is met by a roomful of dour police detectives and his dead wife, strangled by one of his own neck ties. In no time, Henderson is railroaded through the legal system (in a nice sequence of images where only the voice of the prosecutor is heard and the notes of the stenographer are seen) and a date set for his execution for murder. All this despite his insistence that he spent that night with a woman in a funny hat but whose name he never learned. But when every witness insists that he was alone that night, only loyal secretary Carol believes him. Joining forces with a detective with his own doubts and Henderson's partner, Jack Marlow (Franchot Tone), she sets out to prove his innocence. Finally locating the phantom lady and the funny hat, she's elated to be able to prove Henderson's innocence, that is, until she's confronted by the real killer. The plot by Bernard Schoenfeld based on a novel by Cornel Woolrich, moves at a good clip punctuated by scenes that are by turns beautiful and jaw dropping. An example of the first is the entire sequence where Carol follows a bartender witness through the night darkened streets of the city. Every shot is an eye grabber from her silhouette on a misty corner beneath a streetlight, to the empty elevated siding, to the damp sidewalks of the seedy neighborhood where the bartender is struck by a car, to the final shot as the camera pans down from Carol's face to the man's hat lying in the gutter. All done in utter silence except for maybe Carol's clicking heels makes the scenes eerie and suspenseful. The jaw dropping scene is the one where Carol goes undercover as a cheap hotsie totsie and picks up drummer on the make Cliff Milburn (Elisha Cook Jr) hoping he'll tell her the truth about what he saw on the night of the murder. He takes her to a private session where a bunch of sweaty musicians are pounding out some jazz. Milburn takes the bones and starts drumming as Carol stands and sways toward him, getting into the music despite herself. The look on her face and the gestures of her hands in accompaniment to Milburn's wild drumming is as visual an equivalent of orgasm as you're likely to find anywhere in cinema. The scene has to be seen to be believed!

One of Phantom Lady's numerous atmospheric shots

Ella Raines' performance in *The Phantom Lady* may have been somewhat limited, but that still doesn't explain why it took Alan Curtis (Scott Henderson) so long to tumble to her

Elisha Cook Jr as drummer Cliff Milburn sees in Carol Richman what Scott Henderson apparently couldn't!

Laura (1944)

A proto-noir that is really a murder mystery except this time, the dead woman found with her face blasted to pieces, is not the person everyone assumes her to be. The hook here is that the more he researches the life of the supposedly deceased Laura Hunt (Gene Tierney), the deeper in love Det. Mark McPherson (played by Dana Andrews) becomes. Thus, imagine his surprise one night when the dead woman shows up alive and well! Seems someone else was killed that night and therein lies the mystery as McPherson struggles to remain objective when the evidence seems to point to Laura herself. Also in the mix is suave but slimy Shelby Carpenter (Vincent Price) and fay Waldo Lydecker (Clifton Webb). Interestingly, the film, scripted by a whole regiment of 20th Century Fox screenwriters, is narrated by the murderer making for interesting re-viewings once audiences know who he is. However, as McPherson makes his way through a maze of gigolos and sycophants, and justly famous as the mystery is, a number of contrived elements tend to hold the film back from perfection. For instance, is it really likely that the murderer would lug a heavy gauge shotgun through the streets of New York to conveniently make a mess of the face of the woman he kills? Answer: no, it wasn't, but the plot demanded the murdered woman be unrecognizable and the murder weapon, too big to run away with, is hidden in a grandfather's clock, a key element to McPherson's eventually solving the murder. In another place, knowing her life is in danger and warned to lock her door before going to bed, Laura doesn't bother to check the other doors and windows to her apartment thus missing the killer hiding in her kitchen! Other long winded and unlikely explanations by the suspects, though they fit the crime pattern, threaten to collapse under their own weight. Still, director Otto Preminger keeps track of it all with a deft touch with cinematographer Joseph LaShelle providing the looming shadows. The film's final line, "Goodbye my love," should have been the title! There's no noir decision point here, but the film includes other elements that would later become associated with the genre. More than worth a look.

Det. Mark MacPherson (Dana Andrews) sulks as he realizes that he's fallen in love with a dead woman

The painting used in *Laura* didn't do Gene Tierney justice: she photographed much better

Making sure he's not falling in love with a murderess, MacPherson gives Laura the third degree

My Name Is Julia Ross (1945)

Coming in at an economical 65 minutes, this isn't quite a film noir but still intriguing. Stars Nina Foch as the Julia Ross of the title who is desperate to find work while living in England. She finds a position as secretary to a well to do family but when she arrives at the address, is drugged and wakes up a prisoner in a lonely mansion on the coast. As the plot develops, she learns that her employers are trying to convince her she's really another woman, the wife of Ralph Hughes (George Mcready) But Julia isn't having any and after various attempts to escape or get word out to a boyfriend, she learns that Ralph is a homicidal maniac who killed his real wife in a fit of rage. (Indicated to the viewer early on in a scene where Ralph is sitting calmly ripping a pair of Julia's underthings with a knife!) Now, the family is trying to cover up the murder by getting another woman to take the role. The film moves along at a good clip with nice performances by the main cast including Foch and Mcready, and Dame May Whitty as Ralph's mother (she of Hitchcock's *The Lady Vanishes*) Well directed overall by Joseph Lewis (who also helmed the noir classic *Gun Crazy*) there are a couple hitches including a continuity problem involving the switching back and forth of a letter Julia tries to mail and a climax that begs additional footage explaining the surprise ending in which Julia, her boyfriend, and the cops trap Ralph. How was it planned? When did Julia meet with the police to plan the trap? Admittedly, an explanation would have ruined the last minute surprise but by not including it, the viewer can't help but feel a bit cheated. Lewis is ably aided by cinematographer Burnett Guffey who makes most shots fun to look at filled as they are with interesting angles and shadows of the old dark house variety. A fun romp even if it doesn't entirely fit the classic noir formula.

Ralph (George McReady) tears through his dead wife's undies as mother looks on

Prisoner in a gilded cage: Julia Ross is prevented from leaving the Hughes estate

Nina Foch: Pretty good for a mere substitute wife. Murder would be such a waste!

Cornered (1945)

Noirish *Cornered* concerns Canadian war vet Lawrence Gerard (played by Dick Powell) who travels to Argentina in search of Marcel Jarnac, the man responsible for killing his wife execution style in the waning days of World War II. There, after running down a lead to Jarnac's wife, he runs into a web of intrigue involving ex-Vichy French seeking to regain power and former members of the French underground trying to hunt them down. Meanwhile, Gerard connects with Madame Jarnac (Micheline Cheirel) who at first denies any knowledge about her husband still being alive but soon relents. Or so it appears. At the same time, Gerard is lured into the clutches of Senora Camargo (Nina Vale) wife of a wealthy businessman also involved in the intrigue. She tries to seduce him but fails. Nearly framed for murder, Gerard is nevertheless warned by authorities to leave the country but first, he decides to run down one more lead. It's a trap and, in a final twist, he finally comes face to face with Jarnac who, obviously, isn't dead after all. Director Edward Dmytryk manages to keep all of John Paxton and Ben Hecht's twists and turns in the plot in order, just barely, so that attentive viewers can follow the action while cinematographer Harry Wild keeps it all down to earth and matter of fact. Entertaining.

Careful Mr. Gerard! Dick Powell as Lawrence Gerard is romanced by one of the dangerous dames in *Cornered*

On the other hand, falling for Micheline Cheirel might be worth the risk!

Walter Slezak may or may not be the helpful seeming Melchior Incza. Just one of the factors in Paxton and Hecht's complex plot for *Cornered*

Lawrence Gerard finds himself "cornered" in a post-war struggle among ex-Vichy agents and their French underground enemies

Mildred Pierce (1945)

One of the toughest things for Hollywood to do in the 1940s was to adapt a novel by James M. Cain. Along with Raymond Chandler and Dashiell Hammett, Cain was one of the era's top writers of hard boiled crime fiction and even more than his contemporaries, his stories were filled with just the kind of things that Hollywood movies were not allowed to depict...at least not in any overt way. Thus, subjects such as abortion, drug use, and sex had to be treated in a circumspect manner. But such subjects were often integral to Cain's stories making them unavoidable if adapted to film. But somehow, Hollywood's clever screenwriters were able to do it in such a way that their film noirs were often perfectly viewable for the entire family. Case in point: *Mildred Pierce*. Take, for instance, the scene where Veda Pierce (played by Ann Blyth) is negotiating for a divorce from a young millionaire. There, she reveals the shocking news that she's pregnant, squeezing out a last minute $10,000 support fee from the young man's parents. Later, she tells her mother it was all a sham. She married the boy specifically to divorce him and get the cash. Touchy issues like that would be even more difficult to tip toe around in a later Cain adapation: *The Postman Always Rings Twice*. But there was plenty here in *Mildred Pierce* to keep the most prurient imagination satisfied as Mildred (Joan Crawford) sacrifices her first marriage on the altar of devotion to her eldest daughter, the vain, spoiled Veda. Indeed, it's her maniacal devotion to Veda that leads Mildred down the noir path of self destruction as she bankrupts herself, enters a second loveless marriage, is humiliated in the aforesaid divorce proceedings, is accused of murder, and finally is driven to attempted suicide. Mildred's downward course is painful to watch especially in light of Veda's infuriating behavior. Directed by Michael Curtiz, the film never stops, never gives viewers a chance to catch their breaths with cinematography by Ernest Haller providing the atmosphere: scenes in the darkened Beragon beach house as Mildred sets up Wally Fay to take the fall for murder and the silhouetted shot of Veda and Beragon in a clinch before breaking apart and emerging into the light are more than impressive. Casting is good too with Jack Carson's Wally Fay, Ann Blyth's Veda, and especially Eve Arden's sarcastic, tough talking Ida Corwin the standouts. Ranald MacDougall wrote the script adapted from Cain's novel and in doing so, might have actually improved on the source material. His dialouge is crisp and cutting but he saves the best lines for Ida. Spotting Fay checking her out as she straightens out her stockings, Ida tells him: "Leave something on me, I might catch cold!" Yeah, there's a reason why *Mildred Pierce* has been considered a classic for over half a century. Because it is!

Doing Cain one better: Wally Fay (Jack Carson) checks out Ida's gams

Right up Cain's alley: Ann Blythe shows how she fit the role of conniving vixen Veda to a T

James M. Cain

Fallen Angel (1945)

A cross between a proto-noir murder mystery and women's weepy, *Fallen Angel* tells the tale of smooth talking, down on his luck Eric Stanton (played by Dana Andrews) who blows into the little town of Walton and promptly falls madly in love with greasy spoon waitress Stella (Linda Darnell). But then, so's everyone else in town from cafe owner Pop ("Pa Kettle" Percy Kilbride) to ex-cop Mark Judd (Charles Bickford). Only problem is, Eric is flat broke and Stella is tired of one night stands and wants a home with all the trimmings. How to get the money necessary before Stella finds herself another man? Eric sets his sights on local heiress June Mills (Alice Faye) and in a whirlwind courtship, manages to woo her and marry her. But Eric can't shake off his creep nature so that on their wedding night, he abandons his expectant bride to sneak out of the house for a tryst with Stella. That's his noir mistake (added to everything else he's done wrong in the film). The next day Stella is found murdered and he's a prime suspect. The film is flawed by June's puppy dog loyalty to the obviously untrustworthy and backstabbing Eric. Just too unbelievable. But otherwise the film works as a proto-noir with its murder mystery and brutal law enforcement in the form of Judd's kid gloved hands that he uses to beat confessions out of suspects. Joseph LaShelle's cinematography is good (even when the film resorts to sets and rear screen projection) and Otto Preminger's direction is solid in this, one of his three outings with Dana Andrews in the lead. Andrews does it again as the no good Stanton who seems slightly out of his gourd mooning after Darnell when he has Alice Faye already on the line! Bickford is fine as the dirty cop and John Carradine is nicely cast in the brief but fun role of a sophisticated sounding traveling mind reader.

Dead gone for Linda Darnell's slop joint waitress, Stella, Eric Stanton (Dana Andrews) waits for Percy Kilbride's Pop to take a powder

Mark Judd (Charles Bickford) helps out the local constabulary by showing them how the big boys do it back in the city. Here, he slips on the kid gloves before beating a confession out of a murder suspect

Why would Dana Andews' Eric Stanton bother with Linda Darnell when he'd already hooked Alice Faye?

31

Scarlet Street (1945)

Scarlet Street is based on a French novel called *La Chienne* which translates as *The Bitch*, and boy! No story was ever better named! Possibly the very blackest of film noir, *Scarlet Street* follows the decline of an ordinary schlepp who falls in with an attractive street walker (Joan Bennett as Kitty March) who takes him for the ride of his life...all down hill. It begins when Christopher "Chris" Cross (played by Edward G. Robinson) sees a woman being beat up on a darkened street corner. Rushing to her rescue, they strike up an acquaintance during which he allows her to believe that he's a successful painter when actually he's merely a clumsy hobbyist. Enter the woman's boyfriend, the conniving Johnny (Dan Duryea) who gets her to play up to the naive Cross. In no time, Cross is embezzling funds from his employer and stealing money from his nagging wife to fund Kitty's upscale lifestyle. In the meantime, Johnny tries to sell Cross' paintings but with no luck until they're discovered by an art critic. Johnny tells him that Kitty is the painter and suddenly, she becomes the darling of the art world. At the same time, the deceased husband of Cross' wife shows up and Cross is delighted to find that he's now free to marry Kitty. But when he enters her apartment to tell her the good news, he finds Johnny there. Even then, he's prepared to forgive Kitty but she only laughs in his face, calling him a fool. Crushed, Cross loses it and kills Kitty in a rage. He lucks out when the police arrest Johnny for the murder who ends up in the electric chair. Now homeless and unemployable (his embezzlement of company funds was discovered), Cross becomes a bum, sleeping on park benches and haunted by his conscience. He attempts suicide but fails. Now as low as he can go, he passes an art gallery where his paintings are being sold for thousands of dollars but still attributed to Kitty. The final scene in the film shows him as a pathetic figure, shambling along the city streets, completely and totally broken. Directed by Fritz Lang, the film is likely one of his best, certainly his best American film, and one of the earliest and darkest examples of the classic noir formula of ordinary man making one wrong move that initiates a descent that doesn't stop until he hits rock bottom. Robinson was born to play the mousy nebbish Cross and Joan Bennett was perfect as the two faced Kitty who doesn't mind being batted around by her boyfriend. And was Duryea ever so sleazy and scheming as he is here as low life Johnny? Excellent screenplay by Dudley Nichols wastes not a minute in its dizzying downward plunge to abject nihilism for its hapless protagonist. A must see!

Classic scene from *Scarlet Street* symbolizing Chris Cross' debasement. He still has a long way to fall!

Final scene from *Scarlet Street* as the ruined Chris Cross passes gallery where his paintings are being sold for thousands but attributed to the woman who has destroyed his life

Kitty (Joan Bennett) and boyfriend Johnny (Dan Duryea) scheme to milk the naive Cross for all he's worth

The Postman Always Rings Twice (1946)

They said it couldn't be done and they almost didn't do it! That was the popular Hollywood concensus about James M. Cain's novel, *The Postman Always Rings Twice,* with its heaping helpings of adultery, murder, illegitimacy, and betrayal. In fact, the response from the Production Code office stated flatly that the story was "definitely unsuitable for motion picture production." As a result, the property stayed on the shelf for years until screenwriters Harry Ruskin and Niven Busch managed to whip it into presentable shape with all of its more prurient elements addressed obliquely in the script and otherwise left to the viewer's interpretation. Using the black and white photography of Sidney Wagner and selected wardrobe for Cora Smith as played by Lana Turner (she appears on screen either dressed completely in white or completely in black depending on the subject of key scenes) helped in underlining certain action left unspoken (such as illicit sex between the married Cora and randy handyman Frank Chambers played by John Garfield). As for the rest, the pace of events move along swiftly with the hapless Frank falling for Cora at first sight and almost as swiftly, they begin plotting to kill Cora's husband, Nick (Cecil Kellaway). Their first attempt fails but the second doesn't. That's when things begin to fall apart for the sex drunk Frank as hard boiled attorney Arthur Keats (Hume Cronyn) jousts in court with ambitious district attorney Kyle Sackett (Leon Ames). Keats gets the best of Sackett allowing his clients to beat the rap. But now the two love birds, who betrayed each other during the legal proceedings, are at each other's throats. But just as they're reconciled (by way of Cora's revelation that she's carrying Frank's illegitimate child), tragedy strikes. Pretty much as dark as any noir could get, the film hosts few bright spots and what few there are, involve characters living in a fool's paradise. Garfield is good as the smitten sap who falls for Cora's platinum blonde charms. It's easy to believe that he's a guy who keeps his brains in his pants (for instance, his thoughtless, quickie hookup with a woman he meets in a parking lot). While a little too glamorous for the role of Cora, Turner conveys just the right amount of ambition, shallowness, and cold blooded deviousness to be convincing as Nick's dissatisfied young wife. But the film is bolstered with a great cast all around including Cronyn excellent as the shyster lawyer who prizes victory in the courtroom more than justice, Kellaway as the clueless Nick Smith, Alan Reed as the blackmailing private dick, and Ames as the slick district attorney playing off Frank against Cora. All contribute to a downward spiral of self-destruction making this film one of the best in the genre!

Goofy for sex: Frank just can't say no. And who can blame him when Audrey Totter makes the scene?

Frank Chambers (John Garfield) and Cora Smith (Lana Turner) look into the gully having just driven
the hapless Nick Smith to his death

Goofy for sex: Frank (John Garfield) loses his mind after laying eyes on Cora (Lana Turner) for the first
time

The Killers (1946)

Solid early proto-noir film about ex-boxer Pete (the Swede) Lund (Burt Lancaster) who makes "one mistake" and pays for it when he gets drilled by two hit men. Those twenty minutes, which open the movie, are actually its highlight with their combination of restrained direction by Robert Siodmak and diamond sharp cinenmatography by Woody Bredell. Charles McGraw and William Conrad as Al and Max are the torpedo's hired by Big Jim Colfax to ice the Swede who's been hiding out as a garage mechanic in palookaville, New Jersey. The Swede's "mistake" may have been twofold: falling in with a gang planning a payroll robbery and falling in love with bad girl Kitty Collins (Ava Gardner). So far gone is he for Kitty that he takes the rap for her in a stolen jewelry case spending two years in the slammer. When he's finally released, he discovers that Kitty hasn't waited for him. Instead, she's fallen in with Colfax. Still stuck on her, the Swede joins Colfax and his mob for a lucrative payroll heist. Later, when Kitty tells him that his partners intend on cutting him out of his share of the $250,000 haul, he takes pre-emptive action and steals the whole thing for himself. Back at his apartment, Kitty betrays him by taking the loot and deserting him. Knowing his life isn't worth a plugged nickel with the mob, he goes into hiding and it's only sheer coincidence that Colfax finds him on his garage job and sics Al and Max on him. All this is told in bits and pieces as insurance investigator Jim Riordan (Edmond O'Brien) puts it all together. More crime thriller than classic noir with its honest sap who makes that one fatal decision, *The Killers* works beautifully as an early entry into the genre sweepstakes. Based on a short story by Ernest Hemingway, the script by Richard Brooks and others including John Huston is likely an improvement where pitch perfect casting rounds out the excellence. (It was Lancaster's film debut) In fact, only the opening scenes of the Swede's murder is Hemingway's. Everything else is original. Some location shooting adds versimilitude and indoor for outdoor sets work well in this instance to create a certain kind of atmosphere. Quite excellent.

Careful, Burt! She's dynamite!

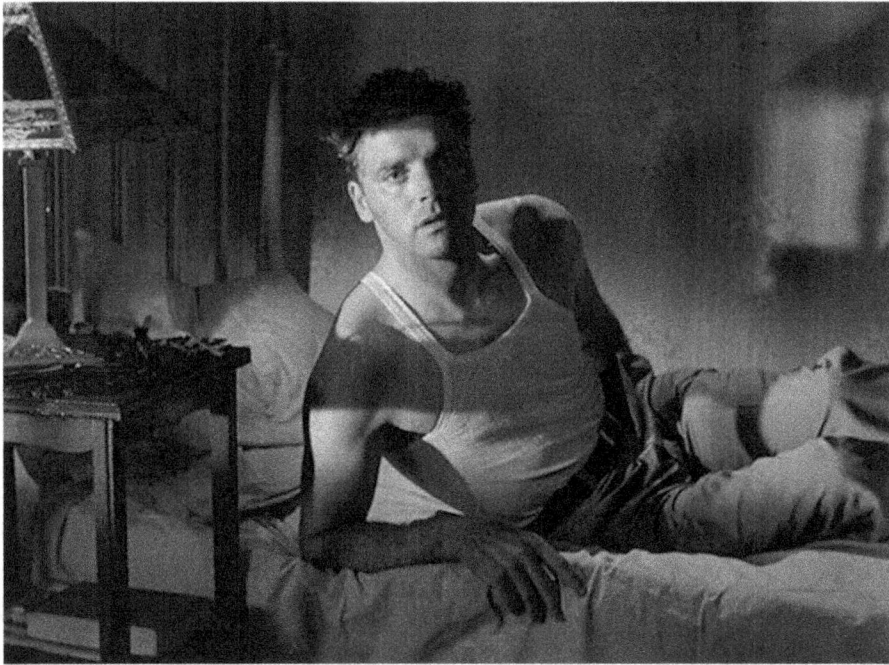

The Swede (Burt Lancaster) is unable to sleep nights never knowing when mob boss Big Jim Colfax will catch up to him

Nice casting: Charles McGraw and William Conrad as Al and Max, torpedos hired by Colfax to off the Swede

Ernest Hemingway

The Dark Corner (1946)

Solid proto-noir with a private eye hero cut from the same cloth as Philip Marlowe or Sam Spade. Mark Stevens is PI with a shady past Bradford Galt now relocated from Frisco to New York with a new office that also comes with a new secretary named Kathleen (Lucille Ball). But Galt's past soon catches up with him in the form of former partner Anthony Jardine (Kurt Kreuger). It seems Galt had caught Jardine with his hand in the cookie jar and in retaliation, Jardine framed him, sending him to prison for two years. Jardine's racket is falling in with rich married women and then blackmailing them. His latest target is Mari Cathcart (Cathy Downs), wife of art dealer Hardy Cathcart (Clifton Webb). But Hardy catches on to his wife's peccadiloes and hires his own private investigator (William Bendix) to try and get the newly arrived Galt to kill Jardine. When that fails, Bendix murders Jardine himself and sets up Galt to take the fall. Now, with only Kathleen on his side and Jardine's body hidden under his bed, Galt is under pressure to discover who tried to frame him before the police catch on. A solid, fast moving murder mystery with all kinds of wrinkles and unexpected twists, the film was directed by Henry Hathaway with gorgeous cinematography by Joseph MacDonald who signals just what kind of movie this was going to be in the opening shots of the darkened stairwell in Galt's office building and in his office itself lit in bands of alternating shadow and light. The baby faced Stevens is deceptive as the tough private eye so that when he explodes in violence it really takes the viewer by surprise. His interaction with Kathleen is also interesting for its risky double entendres and leading talk of seduction. (A scene where a box office clerk overhears them is funny) And while Kathleen's smarmy banter recalls the style mastered by Eve Arden, it tends to fall flat due to the casting of Lucille Ball in the role. Though still somewhat attractive this early in her career, the beginnings of her later, high cheekboned look are apparent to the point the viewer sometimes wonders what Galt sees in her. Much more attractive is Cathy Downs as Mari Cathcart that likely added to Galt's frustration over Jardine! Good one.

Clearly, Cathy Downs had it all over Lucille Ball!

Moody shot from *The Dark Corner*

The bodies keep piling up in *The Dark Corner*!

The Big Sleep (1946)

An all star cast and crew combined to make this film an instant film noir classic! While not involving the tried and true noir formula of regular guy makes one mistake and ends up having his life ruined, *The Big Sleep* covers the other half of that trope: the mystery crime story painted by the cinematographer as a darkened world filled with shadows where nothing is as it appears to be. That's *The Big Sleep* in spades as Philip Marlowe (Humphrey Bogart in tone perfect casting), Lauren Bacall (as slippery Vivian Rutledge), Martha Vickers (as too cute Carmen Brentwood), Louis Jean Heydt (as smooth talking Joe Brody) and especially Bob Steele (as the cold blooded torpedo Lash Canino) combine to form one of the screen's most convoluted murder mysteries. (Legend has it that it was so complicated that one murder was actually never explained...but it was...indirectly) The story is based on the Raymond Chandler novel of the same name that was turned into a script sparkling with cutting dialogue, vivid characterizations, and lightning fast scene changes by the titanic writing trio of William Faulkner, Leigh Brackett, and Jules Furthman. The whole thing is topped off by the direction of screen vet Howard Hawks with top notch cinematography by Sidney Hickox. Interiors as well as exteriors were shot in the studio with excellent period set design. And even though most times doing exterior interiors didn't work, here it does adding an air of unreality to the dual track mysteries that shamus Marlowe finds himself mixed up in. He's hired by rich General Sternwood to fix Joe Brody who's blackmailing him over daughter Carmen's gambling debts and other less savory things but blackmail soon turns into murder and much more as Marlowe is drawn into a world of scheming women, double crossing men, and ruthless killers. Though final edits intended to enhance the Bogart/Bacall relationship may have diluted the results, *The Big Sleep* must be rated as among the top ten noirs of all time.

Even all trussed up, the Bogart/Bacall chemistry was on display throughout *The Big Sleep*

Despite killers like Lash Canino gunning for him and being sweet on Vivian
Rutledge, Spade still found time for a rainy day dalliance with bookstore clerk
(Dorothy Malone). And who could blame him?

It's perfectly obvious here why Joe Brody decided to use Carmen Brentwood (Martha Vickers)
as the subject of his blackmail scheme!

Somewhere In the Night (1946)

John Hodiak is George Taylor, a Marine Corps vet who wakes up in a MASH unit with no memory of who he is. He has one clue to his past life, a note signed by one Larry Cravat that directs him to a bank where cash is waiting for him. More of a proto-noir in that there's no noir decision point but plenty of mystery and atmosphere as Taylor goes from clue to clue while being hounded by underworld figures with local police in the form of Lt. Donald Kendall (Lloyd Nolan) suspicious and hanging onto the margins. He finally finds a person he can trust in the form of nightclub singer Christy Smith (Nancy Guild) who inexplicably falls for him and helps him solve the mystery that is himself. Direction by Joseph Mankiewicz is good as is cinematography by Norbert Brodine. But sets and backlots instead of actual locations spoil things a bit with the film's 110 minute running time a tad too long. Ending is almost predictable involving as it does too slick nightclub owner Mel Phillips (Richard Conte), stolen Nazi loot, and the revelation of Taylor's identity. Good but not earth shattering.

Nightclub singer Christy Smith (Nancy Guild) decides to throw in with John Hodiak as George Taylor; maybe it was his mustache?

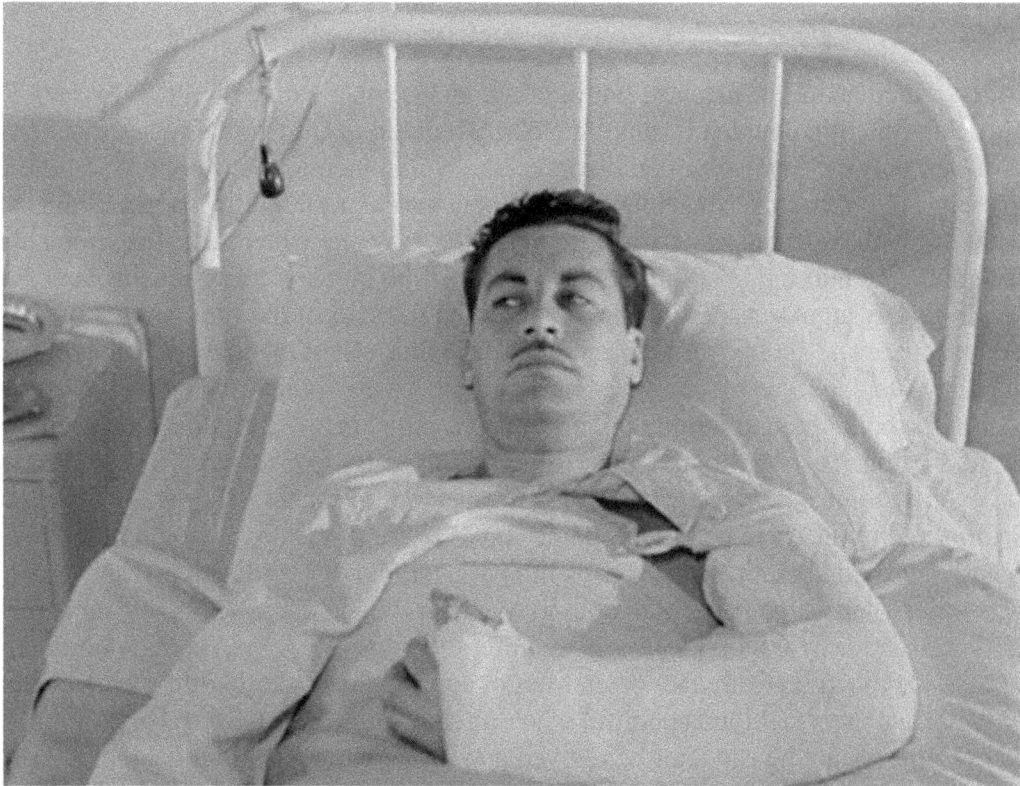

John Hodiak as George Taylor wakes up in a MASH unit with no recollection of his identity

Taylor seeks clues with a fortune teller!

Decoy (1946)

With its often stilted acting, C list cast, flat lighting, and unimaginative direction by Jack Bernhard, one would think that this film couldn't be anything else but a dud as film noir. But surprise! *Decoy* is the kind of noir that only a connoisseur could appreciate. Not to mention viewers with a little imagination as the movie has two centers of focus: Dr. Lloyd Craig and Margot Shelby. While Craig (played by Herbert Rudley) is the noir object of attention in that he's the one who makes the wrong choice and ends up crashing and burning, it's Margot (Jean Gilley) who quickly draws the fascinated attention of the viewer. In fact, Margot gets her just desserts right at the start of the film when a staggering Craig enters her apartment and shoots her before falling dead himself! Why does the dying man kill this attractive young woman? Viewers may well have asked! Turns out that the lady in question is one of the most ruthless, cold blooded femme fatales ever presented in any film noir, first seducing a number of men, including bank robber Frank Olins (Robert Armstrong), gunsel Jim Vincent (Edward Norris), Craig, and even to some extent, Det. Joe Portugal (Sheldon Leonard). All of whom, except the last, she ends up killing with Vincent in particular, being run over after finishing changing the tire on her car! But even with her dying breath, she succeeds in making a fool of Portugal when she asks him to kiss her one last time. Then, as he leans in to comply with her dying wish, she laughs in his face! Bad! As for Craig, he's a doctor with high ideals with a clinic set in the city's poorest neighborhood. A man dedicated to his Hypocratic Oath. But when Margot appears, he instantly falls for her seductress ways (spurning his office nurse, a blond spoonful who's already on the line). She talks him into faking the execution of Olins so that he can later be revived and reveal where he hid the $400,000 stolen in his last heist. The plan works, upon which Craig discovers his true position: a tool for Margot. He was lied to and made an accomplice to murder, a betrayal of his oath as a doctor. His mind shattered, he breaks down into tears. Meanwhile, Margot carries on, killing Olins and then Vincent in turn, she drags Craig to the spot where the money is buried and orders him to dig it up all the while laughing and carrying on in maniacal fashion. Finally, money in hand, she shoots Craig and drives off. But Craig isn't dead, managing to stagger away, hitching a ride into town, and ending the movie where it began. Whew! There was almost nothing like this in the entire history of noir and the screenplay by Nedrick Young is unrelenting. See it to believe it!

Little do they realize, but Edward Norris and Herbert Rudley don't figure in Jean Gillie's plans at all!

Hard to believe a package like this could be so rotten in *Decoy*, but then Jean Gillie did seduce four saps in the course of the film!

Baddest of bad girls, a dying Margot Shelby (Jean Gillie) laughs in the face of Det. Joe Portugal (Sheldon Leonard) after having seduced and killed three other men!

The Blue Dahlia (1946)

Question: how could a film with an original script by hard boiled pulp writer Raymond Chandler (creator of Philip Marlowe) fail to miss? Answer: it can't! Despite fighting his way through an alcoholic haze, Chandler delivered a top notch noir thriller in *The Blue Dahlia* that stars Alan Ladd as ex-Navy pilot Johnny Morrison and Veronica Lake as Joyce Harwood, estranged wife of mobster gone legit Eddie Harwood played by Howard Da Silva. Filled with twists and turns and a stack of murder suspects, Chandler delivers a fast moving, intriguing plot that's peppered with such catchy lines as "Every guy has seen you," Johnny tells Joyce, "the trick is to find you." Or the house dick's line upon finding the body of Johnny's wife and the automatic that killed her: "Suicide? Uh, uh. Too much gun." That, you see, is where it all starts. After Johnny returns home from the Pacific with pals Buzz Wanchek (William Bendix) and George Copeland (a pre-Ward Cleaver Hugh Beaumont) he finds that his wife Helen (Doris Dowling) hasn't exactly been pining over his absence. After arguing over her cozy relationship with Eddie and her having killed their child in a DUI, Johnny splits. But later, when Helen is discovered dead, he becomes the number one suspect. Just by chance, he's picked up along the road by Joyce and they hit it off. After avoiding being rolled in a flophouse racket, Johnny discovers a note by Helen telling of some goods she has on Eddie. Namely, that he's wanted for murder in New Jersey. Confronting the night club owner, Johnny hints of his knowing about the murder rap but before he can do anything with it, he's taken for a ride by a couple of Eddie's henchmen. And when Eddie shows up at the safe house where Johnny is being held, there's a confrontation and Eddie is shot. But by then, Buzz has come clean about his solo visit to Helen before she was killed. He guesses he must have killed her because he'd had one of his frequent blackouts (due to a head injury) and couldn't remember anything of his visit. At least, that's what Chandler had originally wanted for his ending; Buzz being the killer. But the war office objected to a serviceman being a murderer and the ending was changed. Actually for the better as it added yet another layer of complexity to the plot. Director George Marshall does an excellent job with the story and aided by cinematographer Lionel Lindon, manages to capture a mood of apprehension and of walls closing in emblematic of many pulp inspired noirs. (Many of the early scenes are filmed in the rain adding to the film's atmosphere) Naturally, Ladd and Lake are excellent together (despite some justifiable complaints by Chandler about Lake's acting; her delivery is often on the stiff side but then, that was part of her charm) and Bendix is well cast as the dim witted but belligerent army pal. Hugh Beaumont was a semi-regular in film noir through the forties and fifties, usually as a calming factor in the plot as friend of the protagonist or sympathetic police detective and he's good here. All together a must see for the noir fanatic!

William Bendix as Buzz Wanchek, Hugh Beaumont as George Copeland, and Alan Ladd as Johnny Morrison

Veronica Lake

The suspects gather: did Buzz do it? That's how writer Raymond Chandler wanted it but not the War Department! Johnny would have to keep looking

Night Editor (1946)

Tony Cochrane (William Gargan) has made a mistake. He's fallen for one of the baddest of bad girls in the form of curvacious Jill Merrill (Janis Carter), the wife of a rich geezer. But Tony is also married, to the long suffering Martha. Though early in the noir trend, *Night Editor* follows the soon to become familiar classic formula as Tony goes from one crisis to the next all following on the heels of that first wrong step. It starts when he witnesses a murder while at a lovers' lane with Jill. So far so good. He could just walk away right? Wrong! Because Tony is also a homicide detective who finds himself assigned to the case! Guilt over his adulterous affair with Jill combines with his sense of duty to find the killer but hopefully without the need of revealing the fact that he was a witness. Just when he thinks he has the cat back in the bag, Jill throws him a curve by claiming she was with the killer the night of the murder, providing him with an alibi. Meanwhile, an innocent man has been charged with the crime putting more pressure on Tony's conscience. He finds the evidence that will prove Jill's lie but to do so will mean revealing his role in the case ruining his career and maybe meaning jail time. But not to worry! Martha, who's suspected her husband had been cheating all the time, forgives him. The film has it both ways with the noir formula: redemption for Tony but also punishment. His marriage is saved but he ends up running a canteen on the ground floor of a great metropolitan newspaper! Which is how the night editor of the title knows about him and is able to recount his story to viewers. Gargan's portrayal of Tony is on the bland side. So much so that one wonders what Jill saw in him? For her part, Janis Carter as Jill is believably bad. Besides being an adulteress, she possesses a sick mind. First, she expresses the perverse desire to look upon the murder victim's bashed in skull then hooks up with her murderer! Brrrr! It all qualifies Janis Carter as a candidate for the femme fatale hall of fame. Director Henry Levin does a decent job staying out of the way of the plot but the script by Hal Smith includes a questionable time element involving Tony's last minute confession to halt the innocent man's date with an electric chair. Did it really take only a few days to go from being arrested to execution? At a mere 68 minutes, you can't get more economical than this little thriller!

Lovely Janis Carter proved too much for bland William Gargan to handle

48

Better times:Jill Merrill plays along with lover Tom Cochrane...before lowering the boom

Tom Cochrane (back to camera) meets with his boss on the scene to investigate a murder he witnessed the night before when making out with Jill

Deadline at Dawn (1946)

Deadline at Dawn was a different kind of noir in that it seemed to be an uneasy melding of light hearted romcom and deadly seriousness when a naive sailor on shore leave teams up with a dance hall floozie to find a killer and keep the sailor from being blamed for the murder. Sailor Alex Winkley (played by Bill Williams) wakes up after a night of drinking with a wad of cash on his person. Slowly, he begins to remember that he'd been up in the apartment of Edna Bartelli (Lola Lane), a local call girl with a long list of clients. Meanwhile, cynical dance hall girl June Goffe (Susan Hayward) finds his naivete refreshing and takes him home with her. There, he fills her in on the money and she accompanies him back to Edna's apartment in order to return it. When they arrive, they find Edna dead. Believing that Alex is innocent, June decides to help him find the killer by backtracking his possible movements. This eventually leads them to a number of suspects including a young husband who'd been seeing Edna behind his wife's back, a blind piano player who was actually Edna's husband, and one of Edna's clients who happens to know her brother, the thuggish Val Bartelli (Joseph Calleia). Alex and June are eventually aided by a wise cab driver until everything comes out in the wash: a shock reveal and Alex and June becoming an item. Director Harold Cluman does a good job keeping screenwriter Clifford Odets' often convoluted plot and its myriad characters clear and moving forward while Nicholas Masuraca's cinematography holds the film firmly in noir territory with the innocent sailor being swept up in a tide of murder and sex. Although the film is well cast, the two standouts that provide it with a double shot of adorability are a youthful Susan Hayward and newcomer Osa Massen as Helen Robinson, the young wife with a cheating husband. A good proto-noir mystery that holds together well, *Deadline at Dawn* is worth any afficionado's time!

The body count rises in *Deadline at Dawn*

Nothing to sneeze at: Why Susan Hayward's June Goffe took a shine to Alex Winkley's Bill Williams is anyone's guess!

Bill Williams (Alex Winkley) tells June Goffe (Susan Hayward) about waking up in a room with a murdered woman and a wad of cash in his pocket: Will she buy it?

Shock (1946)

Rather slight proto-noir in which psychiatrist Richard Cross (Vincent Price) is spotted murdering his wife by pretty war bride Janet Stewart (Anabel Shaw) who promptly goes into *Shock*. (The movie's title, get it?) The next morning, her husband a freshly discharged Lt. Paul Stewart (Frank Latimore) arrives on the scene to find his young wife immobilized. The hotel doctor remembers that there's a top psychiatrist on the premises and what do you know? It's Cross! Cross recommends Janet be taken to his sanitarium where he intends on making her condition permanent. But Janet refuses to cooperate, reviving from time to time to rave about Cross murdering his wife. No one believes her of course but taking no chances, Cross and his scheming mistress, nurse Elaine Jordan (Lynn Bari) plan to pump Janet full of drugs and kill her. A proto-noir, Cross here makes the mistake of killing his wife and not going immediately to the police (as he laments later in the film after he's in too deep). From that point on, goaded by nurse Jordan, he makes one bad decision after another until there's nothing left but the gallows. (Or the electric chair as the case may be) A fun tale of sanitarium shenanigans lit mostly by its attractive co-stars: the sultry Bari and the adorable Shaw. The film was to have been directed by Henry Hathaway (instead, we got nobody Alfred Werker) who might have been able to lift it from so-so status to something with some actual meat on its bones. Oh, well.

What Anabel saw: Namely, Dr. Richard Cross in the act of killing his wife

Lynn Bari as nurse Elaine Jordan just may have been worth killing for!

Reverse angle: Anabel (Janet Stewart) reacts as she witnesses the murder that will send her into *Shock!*

Mike Shayne Mysteries (1946)

Not quite true film noir, the Mike Shayne Mystery series was a popular franchise for Twentieth Century Fox before it was taken over by poverty row studio Producers Releasing Corporation. The series began with Lloyd Nolan in the title role before Hugh Beaumont took over for PRC. Those included *Murder is My Business, Larceny in Her Heart, Blond for a Day, Three On a Ticket,* and *Too Many Winners.* Although the films each featured tightly wound mysteries involving tried and true noir elements such as the femme fatale who walks in the door kicking off the story and bodies turning up when least expected, they failed in their lack of technique. Filming was so rushed (in fact, all of Beaumont's films were shot in a single year!) that directors and cinematographers had little or no time to get creative. The results were films shot in a no frills straight ahead fashion (albeit much of the time on location in the Los Angeles area which helped muchly in creating a sense of accidental versimilitude) with mostly flat lighting. Acting was decent if perfunctory with a pre-*Leave It to Beaver* Beaumont the best of the bunch. Beaumont managed to give Shayne an easy going style as he appeared to relax under police grilling or joking while being slugged by the bad guys. His cool demeanor was underscored by Shayne's habit of casually munching on peanuts. Although Shayne's character differentiated himself from other hard boiled dicks by being slugged at least twice in every film and having little use for a gat, he could give as well as he got when given the chance which, uniquely, wasn't that often. Shayne relied more on his brains than his brawn. Shayne's easy going style was bolstered by some light comic relief in the form of long suffering secretary and ostensible love interest, Phyllis Hamilton. Fun.

Mystery writer Brett Halliday was the creator of Mike Shayne, filling his novels with all the sort of things that Hollywood adaptations of his work could only hint at

Cherryl Walker was only one of several actresses who played Shayne's long suffering secretary Phyllis Hamilton

Mike Shayne (Hugh Beaumont) about to get one of the beatings he routinely endured in order to complete the jobs he was hired for

Born to Kill (1947)

The great Lawrence Tierney plays Sam Wilde, an insane, misanthropic social climber who lets nothing and no one get in the way of what he wants including best friend and keeper, Marty Waterman (Elisha Cook Jr). In a quickie film by director Robert Wise that explores the extent of human falibility, the usual noir protagonist switches gender. In this case, it's divorcee Helen Brent (Clair Trevor) who takes a wrong turn and pays the ultimate price. Her mistake is falling for steely eyed but oddly magnetic Sam who bulldozes his way into her affections and then, when balked at breaking up with her new fiance for him, shifts to her pretty young foster sister, Georgia (Audrey Long). But there's trouble in paradise when not only Helen but Marty both move in to live under the same roof as Sam and Georgia. Furthermore, Helen just can't shake her fascination for Sam despite having discovered that he's responsible for two murders back in Reno. Jealous of her sister, she tries to resist Sam's allure but can't. In one scene, she loses control and throws herself into Sam's arms while a description of his bloody murders throws them both into an orgiastic fervor. Whew! Later, when Marty speaks to Helen alone, trying to convince her to stay away from his volatile friend, Sam spots him leaving her room. In a jealous rage, he even interrupts Marty's attempted murder of Mrs. Kraft (Esther Howard) that he himself had asked him to do. (Kraft hired a private detective to find the killer of one of her tenants whom Sam killed at the start of the film, also in a jealous rage). Sam kills Marty thus allowing Kraft to escape. When Marty's murder is discovered, both Helen and Georgia's first instinct is to protect Sam from the police even with the realization that he's responsible for at least three murders! Finally, shocked by how far Georgia will go for Sam, Helen turns on him herself. When he learns of her betrayal...well, that would be telling! Suffice it to say, in the best noir style, Helen pays dearly for straying from the straight and narrow.

In a jealous rage, Sam Wilde (Lawrence Tierney) takes out friend and handler Marty Waterman (Elisha Cook Jr)

**Georgia (Audrey Long) is used by Sam as a way
to stay close to sister Helen**

**Laurie Palmer (Isabel Jewel) spots the body of her boyfriend on the kitchen floor just before she's done in by
a jealous Sam thus kicking off the events that will eventually catch up to the killer**

Lady in the Lake (1947)

You can't go wrong adapting the work of any of the *Black Mask Detective* authors and so Robert Montgomery doesn't here for *Lady in the Lake*, an adaptation of Raymond Chandler's novel of the same name. With clever, clipped dialogue supplied by screenwriter Steve Fisher (also a *Black Mask* alumnus), the film captures the hard boiled spirit of the pulp detectives as Phillip Marlowe finds his way through a bewildering maze of murders, betrayals, and deceptions to finally solve a case in which he's hired first by one person, quits, and then is hired by another. Surprisingly, Chandler himself had written a script for the film but it was turned down in favor of Fisher's rewrite which shortened the story and set the action at Christmastime resulting in the incongruous opening sequence in which the credits are given on a stack of Christmas cards as carols are sung in the background. When the last card is taken away, a gun is revealed. That segues directly to a shot of Robert Montgomery (as Phillip Marlowe) sitting in his office introducing the story. The film was Montgomery's first solo directorial effort and for it, he chose a risky way of telling the story: completely from the point of view of the subjective camera. Narrated by Marlowe, the character would rarely be seen on camera except for brief glimpses in mirrors and quick shots back to his office. But studio execs' fears were groundless. The movie made a decent profit and the former ingenue went on to other directorial triumphs, but not at the same studio. Anyway, Montgomery is supported in his role as Marlowe by blond bombshell Audrey Totter (playing Adrienne Fromsett who unfortunately for her admirers, leaves her hair up for most of the picture) the untrustworthy magazine editor who hires the detective to find the missing wife of her publisher. Lloyd Nolan does a believable job playing the corrupt police Lt. DeGarmot and Jayne Meadows is suitably hysterical as Mildred Haveland, the rotten apple of DeGarmot's eye. *Woman in the Lake* is an engaging, fast moving mystery of the proto-noir period. The only drawback being that the subjective camera creates the sense that the film is composed as a string of interviews as characters stare into the camera and react to questions from the unseen Marlowe. But never mind that. This one's definitely a must see! **Fun Fact:** "Ellay Mort" is credited as Chrystal Kingsby but there's no such person. The dead woman never makes an appearance in the film. The name Ellay Mort is a play on the French phrase "Elle est Morte," translated as "She is dead!"

**One of the few times in *Lady in the Lake* when viewers catch a glimpse of the star.
That's Robert Montgomery in the mirror and lucky for us, Audrey Totter lets her hair
down for this scene!**

Audrey Totter didn't appear in nearly enough noirs to satisfy fans!

Jayne Meadows played the ditzy Mildfed Haveland who's caught at a murder scene by Marlowe

Tough cop Lloyd Nolan looks on as his boss tries to deal with a cranky (and off screen) Philip Marlowe

Dark Passage (1947)

Following in the footsteps of *Lady in the Lake,* a film that was released in January of 1947, *Dark Passage* opens with a subjective camera trick in which viewers are shown only what escaped con Vincent Parry (played by Humphrey Bogart) sees through his own eyes. That POV begins intriguingly from inside a metal drum after it comes to a rest at the bottom of a ravine. From it, emerges Parry to the sound of warning sirens from nearby San Quentin. In fact, the first half of the movie is shown mostly from Parry's point of view as he's rescued by Irene Jansen (Lauren Bacall) and taken to her apartment. Turns out she was a sympathetic observer at his trial for the murder of his wife who just happened to come across him as he's hiding in the brush. From that initial contact, the pieces of the mystery of just who really did kill his wife fall into place as Parry is framed for the murder of a friend named George Felsinger, blackmailed by a two bit hood, dodges the police, and finally runs down the culprit. Aside from meeting Irene, the only other thing that goes right for Parry is meeting a helpful cab driver who directs him to an underground physician who changes his face so that he goes from looking like Kenneth MacDonald (who starred most famously as "Mr. Slip" in Three Stooges shorts) to Humphrey Bogart! For a famous actor and the big draw of *Dark Passage*, Bogart's face isn't seen in the movie until well past the half way point as first he's only indicated from a subjective camera angle and later has his face covered in bandages following surgery. Lauren Bacall is good as Irene but toned down considerably from her white hot performance in *To Have and Have Not*. Agnes Moorehead as Madge Rapf is suitably unlikeable but miscast as a jealous former girlfriend of Bruce Bennett, who plays Irene's current amour. That is, before Bogart makes the scene! But Houseley Stevenson as Dr. Walter Coley steals the show as the cynical disgraced surgeon who takes pride in his work.
Director/screenwriter Delmar Daves keeps things moving forward taking full advantage of San Francisco locations particularly iconic shots of the Golden Gate Bridge. The Streamline Moderne Malloch Building was used as the location of Irene's apartment and surely made for a striking set with its outdoor elevator and nautical looking lines. The film has a mixed ending: Vincent and Irene get together but only in Peru as Vincent is still wanted for the murder of George Felsinger! That said, *Dark Passage* is worth an investigation by any fan of noir.

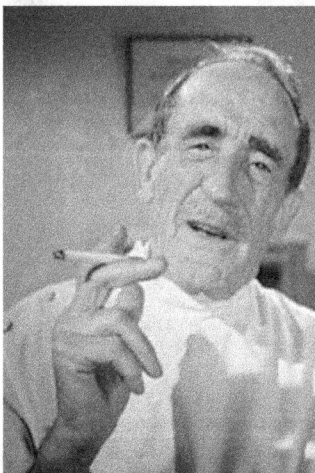

Houseley Stevenson almost steals the show as the discredited Dr. Walter Coley who gives Vincent Parry a new face

From Kenneth MacDonald...

...to Humphrey Bogart! It was convenient keeping Bogart's face hidden until after his surgery obviating the need say, of having MacDonald play him for the first half of the movie!

Location shooting around San Francisco went a long way to establishing the versimilitude of *Dark Passage*

Kiss of Death (1947)

Two time loser Nick Bianco (played by Victor Mature, he of the sleepy eyes) is caught attempting to rob a jewelry exchange and sent to Sing Sing. But before he goes up the river, he's approached by Assistant DA Louis D'Angelo (Brian Donlevy) who offers him a deal: suspended sentence in return for some sqealing. Nick compounds his noir decision point (his first bad move came when he decided to rob the jeweler) by refusing to cooperate. But when he learns that his wife has committed suicide and his children have been placed in an orphanage, he has a change of heart. Dealing with D'Angelo, he's released and goes undercover to get the goods on underworld hit man Tommy Udo (Richard Widmark in his breakthrough role). He succeeds and for a while all is sweetness and light: he's reunited with his kids and marries the sweet young thing (Colleen Grey) who'd first given him the news about his family while he was in prison. Then the case against Udo collapses and now Nick fears not only for his own life but those of his family. With the police unable to do anything about Udo unless they catch him in the act, Nick confronts the creepy hitman goading him into shooting him after notifying D'Angelo. In the best noir style, Nick ends up pumped full of lead but survives to live happily ever after. (Although the original ending did see him die) With narration by Grey's Nettie (the film was also Grey's first credited role), the film unwinds as a docu-drama with veteran director Henry Hathaway's sure hand at the tiller. A good cast is everything for pictures like this and *Kiss of Death* has that but really struck gold with Widmark whose smarmy voice, crooked toothy smile, and vicious, unpredictable ways instantly captures the attention. (Widmark said he based his portrayal of Udo on Batman bad guy the Joker) The scene where he shoves a woman in a wheelchair down a staircase is justly notorious, one that would stereotype Widmark as a ruthless hood for years.

In one of the most infamous scenes in the history of noir, Richard Widmark as Tommy Udo, shoves a wheelchair bound woman down a flight of stairs to her death. He did it because she claimed she didn't know the whereabouts of her son whom Udo was looking for

With his toothy smirk, Richard Widmark as Tommy Udo does bear a resemblance to the Joker; throw in the hat and overcoat and the resemblance is even closer to the 70s Steve Englehart/Marshall Rogers version

Tommy Udo takes a parting shot at Nick Bianco at the climax of *Kiss of Death*

T-Men (1947)

Hard edged procedural directed by Anthony Mann that manages the rare quality of transferring to the viewer a real sense of peril for its protagonists. For sure, a key element in its threatening, edge of the seat suspense, is the great Charles McGraw (as mob hitman Maxie) whose every move is loaded with menace made all the more palpable by John Alton's incredible cinematography. McGraw's craggy no nonsense features are no better served than the close up used in a steam room scene just before he murders the Schemer (Wallace Ford) where Alton fairly sculpts his face in light and shadow. In another scene loaded with tension, as Maxie shoots undercover Treasury agent Tony Genaro (Alfred Ryder), partner Dennis O'Brien (Dennis O'Keefe) looks on unable to speak or act without blowing his own cover and being killed himself. All he can do is lower his head in helpless frustration, the brim of his fedora slowly drawing a shadow over his features. Alton's skill is displayed right off the bat in the film's opening scene where Treasury officials plan the undercover operation that O'Brien and Tony will embark upon in order to uncover a counterfeiting ring. There, Alton manages to show reflections of everyone at the meeting in the shiny surface of the meeting room table! From there, the script by John Higgins takes the agents into the seamy underworld where they soon pick up the trail of a small time crook named the Schemer who leads them to the lower rungs of the counterfitting operation. But every step of the way, Mann makes sure to underline the fact of how dangerous what the agents are doing is and that sense of suspense never lets up for the whole movie right until the final minutes when O'Brien waits, hoping a final gambit will spare his life. Of course McGraw is top notch and so is the cool headed O'Keefe. But keep an eye out for Jane Randolph (*Cat People*) as the sang froid second in command of the counterfit ring, June Lockhart (*Lost in Space*) as Tony's wife who inadvertently gives his identity away, and in a very brief non-credited role, John Newland, of *One Step Beyond* fame. Does it need to be said? If you don't see this one, you'll never be able to hold your head up again among noir afficionados!

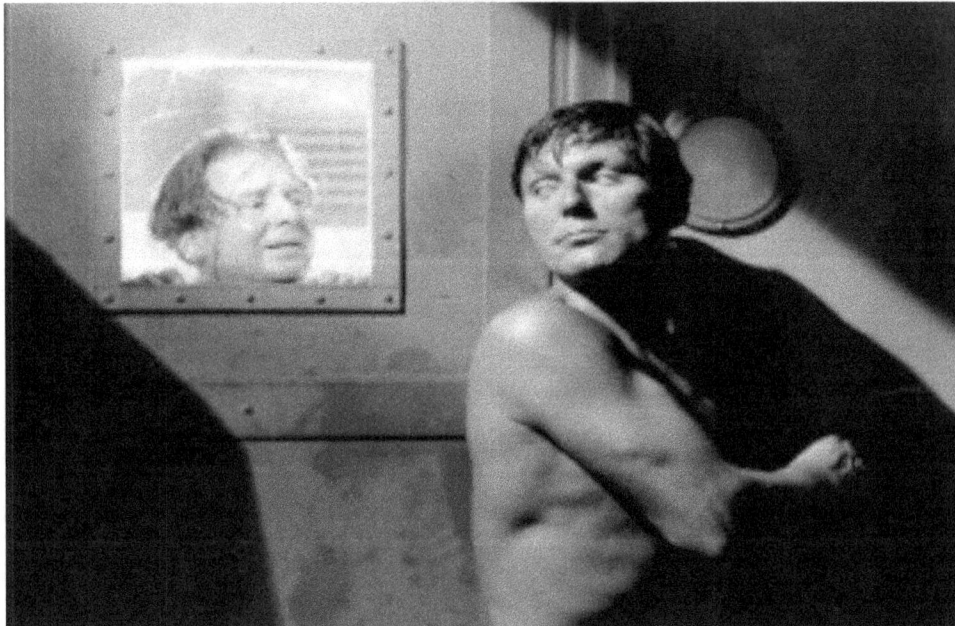

**Lit by John Alton, Charles McGraw (as mob hitman Maxie) offs Wallace Ford's
Schemer by pressure cooking him in the steam room**

As nightclub photographer Evangeline, you couldn't pick a better come on girl than Mary Meade!

In one of the film's most intense moments, Dennis O'Brien (Dennis O'Keefe) can only watch as partner Tony Genaro is killed by the mob after being ID'd as a T-Man

Railroaded (1947)

Tight, fast paced, part police procedural, part straight film noir as innocent waif is framed for the murder of a policeman during the robbery of a bookie joint. The waif is Steve, the brother of attractive Rosie Ryan (played by Sheila Ryan), a laundry delivery man whose truck was used in the robbery. Evidence quickly mounts against Steve as police first identify his truck, then his scarf used as a mask during the robbery. Add the fact that one of the gunmen was wounded and on his deathbed fingers Steve as his partner. The lack of an alibi seems to seal the deal as police detectives eager to send a cop killer to the gas chamber virtually "railroad" the innocent Steve. Meanwhile, the real killer, Duke Martin (John Ireland), schemes behind the back of his boss, classy, poetry spouting club owner Jackland Ainsworth (Roy Gordon). In fact, Martin conspired with girlfriend Clara Calhoun (Jane Randolph) to rob one of Ainsworth's bookie operations. Now, one by one, Martin begins to kill off anyone who might point the finger at him, including Clara whom he's hidden away in a dingy apartment to make sure she doesn't spill the beans. But having doubts about the suspect's guilt, police detective Mickey Ferguson (Hugh Beaumont) uncovers clues that lead to Martin as the actual killer. Expertly directed by Anthony Mann with cinematography by Guy Roe, the story moves right along first as evidence is gathered against Steve and then shifting among departments at precinct headquarters as tests are run on the bullets used in the murder and parafin tests for gun powder residue. From there, the story moves into a budding romance between Mickey and Rosie and then Rosie and the scheming Martin. It's through Martin that Rosie becomes involved more directly in the action and leads to one of the picture's most memorable sequences in which Rosie and Clara go woman to woman in an action packed cat fight as Martin secretly looks on. In fact, Randolph's portrayal of Clara as being at once tough and wisecracking under a police grilling but pathetically clinging to Martin in a hopeless love affair even as he slaps her around turns out to be the best performance in the film. Not to sleight Beaumont of course. His performance as the cool, tough, businesslike police detective is good too, a persona he used often in other noir roles throughout his early career. (Before taking on his most memorable role as Ward Cleaver) All together, *Railroaded,* though a minor entry in the noir cannon, looms large as one of its more successful entries.

At police headquarters, innocent laundry man Steve Ryan is *Railroaded* by detectives eager to put one in the win column

As Rosie Ryan, Sheila Ryan gave Det. Mickey Fergusson plenty of reason to try and clear her brother!

Railroaded gets rolling after the robbery of a bookie fronted by a beauty parlor
operated by Clara Calhoun

Out of the Past (1947)

Quintessential noir with Robert Mitchum as small town garage owner Jeff Bailey who's a sucker for a pretty face. Bailey is really Jeff Markham, formerly a slightly shady private detective now on the lam hoping to escape the notice of mob boss Whit Sterling (Kirk Douglas). Sterling, it seems, was shot by his girlfriend who then absconded with a cool $40,000 in cash. But Sterling's lust for Kathie Moffat (a smoking hot Jane Greer) is greater than his desire for retribution. All he wants is to get her back. So he hires Markham to find her. He does but as soon as Markham sets eyes on Kathie, he forgets all about Sterling. Lust knocks all common sense out of him. She professes innocence about the money and hating Sterling. Markham, totally blinded by the girl's charms, believes her and they end up on the run together until the night when Markham's partner Jack Fisher (noir fave Steve Brodie) finds them keeping house in San Francisco. Threatened with blackmail, Markham ends up in a fight with him until Fisher is shot down by Kathie who then disappears leaving behind a bankbook indicating that she did steal the $40,000. That's when a disillusioned Markham buries himself in Bridgeport...until Sterling finds him. Professing no hard feelings, the mobster says all he wants is for Markham to do one little job for him. But it's a set up. Markham guesses the truth while at the same time finding just how untrustworthy and calculating Kathie could be. Dense, complicated, multi-layered and as noir as noir could be, *Out of the Past* is what might be called the perfect film noir or otherwise! Although director Jacques Tourneur creates a masterpiece of suspense and intrigue, it's tempting to have him share the credit with Nicholas Masuraca whose cinematography is indispensable to the success of the film. Masuraca works miracles as he sculpts Mitchum's fedora and trenchcoated figure in shadow and light making for a number of amazingly moody scenes that capture the essence of forties noir. Mitchum himself is perfectly cast as the melancholy Markham who's at once sympathetic and hard boiled. The scene where he walks into a nightclub office and slugs the manager with barely a thought before calmly helping himself to a cigarette from the unconscious man's desk provides all the viewer needs to know about his tough guy personality. And Greer! When she makes her first entrance at the Mexican cantina in white form fitting dress and big panama style hat with Masuraca's back lighting, well suffice it to say, every male in the audience understood exactly why Sterling didn't care that he was almost killed by her or how cynical, world weary Markham could fall for her hook line and sinker! A must see for every self respecting movie fan and not just noir addicts!

The scheming Kathy looks on hoping to see Jeff Markham and Jack Fisher take each other out

Jane Greer hardly needed any enhancement by the wardrobe department to drive men such as Jeff Markham or Whit Sterling mad!

Even though she's tried to kill both of them, Whit Sterling (Kirk Douglas) and Jeff Markham (Robert Mitchum) can't let Kathie go

Nightmare Alley (1947)

A true film noir that details how far the protagonist can fall after hitting bottom without being killed! In this case, Stan Carlisle's (Tyrone Power) fate is foreshadowed in the very first minutes of the film as he wonders about the pathetic case of a sideshow geek he sees running and screaming madly as he's chased down by his keepers. Shudder! Carlisle is an ambitious circus roustabout who seduces mind reader Zeena Krumbein (Joan Blondell) into sharing with him the secret of her act after disposing of her drunken husband through alcohol poisoning. On the side, he cheats with sideshow performer Molly (Colleen Grey) whom he's eventually forced to marry. Leaving the circus, he uses the mind reading tricks he's learned to set himself up as a phony revivalist before falling in with an equally phony female psychiatrist (Helen Walker). Using the psychiatrist's recordings of her rich clientele, Stan stands to swindle millions out of the credible boobs. But then it all goes south and suddenly, he's on the run from the law, takes to drinking, and becomes a homeless, alcoholic hobo. In desperation, he crawls back to a local circus begging for work, any kind of work. And wouldn't you know it? He's offered the only opening on the lot: the role of geek! Then, one night, when Stan finds himself in the same screaming, running mania that he saw the geek doing at the very start of the story (kept in booze by management, a geek was supposed to act the part of a beast biting the heads off chickens, rats, and anything else the audience suggested...ugh), that he bumps into Molly, who just happens to be working at the same circus. Emerging from his madness for a second, Stan recognizes her and as they embrace, viewers are led to think that there might be salvation for Stan. Too bad! Jules Furthman's script tells the tale of a young man with a golden tongue who seduces, kills, cheats, and even offends Heaven in his pursuit of wealth. In other words, Stan deserves everything he gets...and more! It was a scenario director Edmund Goulding pictured in no uncertain terms with cinematographer Lee Games doing excellent work on nighted circus grounds (which the studio built from scratch across 40 acres with genuine sideshow attractions to keep things authentic), sleazy hotel rooms, and shadow haunted groves dedicated to the dear departed. Power is great as the man the viewer will love to hate, cast perfectly as the irresistably handsome and golden tongued swindler. Blondell is well cast too as the sometimes boozy end of her career sideshow act. Both Grey (whom Stan takes for granted) and Walker (whom he resists so as not to jeopardize his act) are attractive enough to make the viewer wonder how Power's Stan could possibly resist their charms. A winner all around and a true, first class, noir!

Director Edmund Goulding foreshadows Stan Carlisle's fate

Stan Carlisle was too busy conning his way to the top to give much notice to Colleen Grey

Stan Carlisle works his charms on Zeena Krumbein (Joan Blondell)

Crossfire (1947)

After a strong opening, *Crossfire* retreats into a pair of flashbacks as told by soldiers involved in the murder of a Jewish man. In the first, Montgomery (played by Robert Ryan) tells his version of how he and his army buddies ended up in the apartment of Joseph Samuels (Sam Levene) just before he was killed. An even lengthier recollection was then made by Arthur Mitchell (George Cooper), an emotionally disturbed soldier whose story about meeting a girl at a dance hall and then crashing in her apartment is less than convincing. Wanting to believe him though are his sergeant, Peter Keeley (Robert Mitchum), his wife Mary (Jacqueline White), and police detective Finlay (Robert Young). Key to proving Mitchell's story rests with dance hall girl Ginny Tremaine (Gloria Graham) who at first refuses to admit she knows him. That's later blown out of the water when her husband shows up saying that indeed Mitchell had been in the apartment. But all that was beside the point (at least to viewers...and as would be shown later in the film, to Finlay) as, early in the movie, under questioning by the police, Montgomery hints at being prejudiced against Jews. That, and Robert Ryan himself who made a career of portraying unlikable, patronizing, wiseguys were dead giveaways. Ryan presents his usual screen persona here at first acting all innocent and unknowing to authorities and then menacing and dangerous in private. Mitchum is pretty low key and Young is good as the cool, knowing Finlay. Noir favorite Graham is perhaps at her voomiest as a dance hall girl and though she was usually stuck playing the unlucky wife, White could sure make it seem as if her husbands at least were lottery winners! Directed by Edward Dmytryk, the film moves right along in mostly police procedural style while underplaying its ugly anti-semitic through line. A lengthy speech by Young near the conclusion puts it all into focus while cinematography by J. Roy Hunt keeps the atmosphere properly noir. Every scene seems to take place at night or in darkened interiors like movie theaters and dingy hideouts. In fact, the film opens on a fight in an apartment where the contestants are mostly shown as shadows on the wall until a lamp is knocked over plunging the scene into darkness. Somewhat pedantic at times, but worth a gander.

At his smarmy, ingenuous best, Robert Ryan as Montgomery tries to soft pedal Peter Keeley (Robert Mitchum) and Det. Finlay (Robert Young) during an interrogation

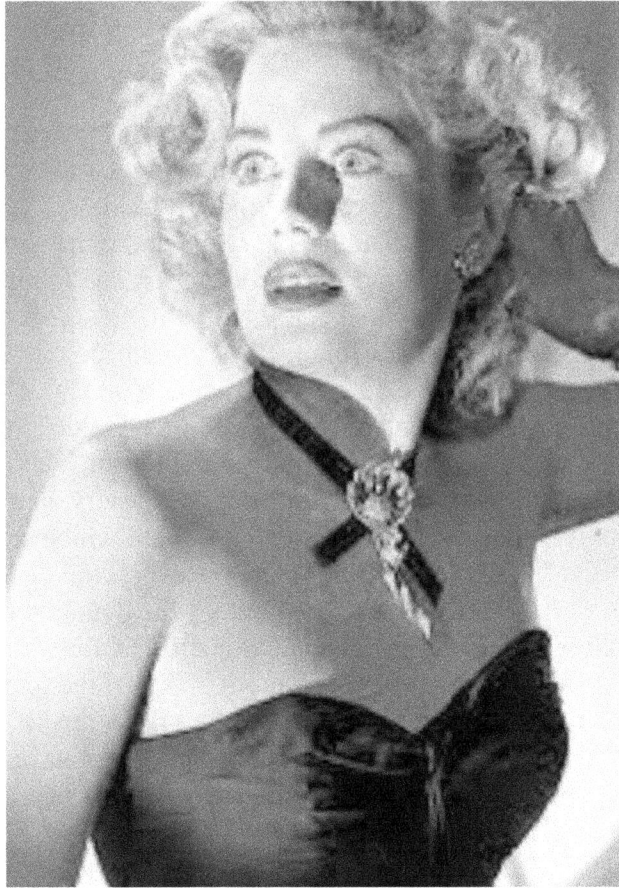

Jacquiline White was usually cast as wives or girlfriends but clearly, she was suited for much more!

When Jacqueline met Gloria: Mary Mitchell convinces Ginny Tremaine to come clean

Johnny O'Clock (1947)

The oddball name for this film's lead character, Johnny O'Clock (Dick Powell), is remarked upon several times during the movie but its inherent humor is in stark contrast to the no nonsense Johnny who operates on the fringes of the law. He's the partner of underworld boss Guido Marchettis (Thomas Gomez) in the ownership of a gambling casino. But he soon falls under the scrutiny of Det. Koch (Lee J. Cobb) in his search for dirty cop Chuck Blaydon who wants to replace Johnny at the club. Blaydon ends up dead along with hat check girl Harriet Hobson (Nina Foch), an apparent suicide. But Koch discovers she was actually murdered and suspects Johnny. Meanwhile, Johnny has fallen hard for Harriet's sister Nancy (Evelyn Keyes) but when he suspects that he's on Guido's target list due to incriminating evidence that suggests he's romantically involved with Guido's wife (Ellen Drew), Johnny deliberately gives Nancy the cold shoulder. But now Nancy's stuck and in the climax of the film, defends Johnny against the clutches of the law. Half murder mystery, half romance, *Johnny O'Clock* is a tightly told puzzler with lots of moving parts not least of which are the unusual number of attractive women hovering around Johnny including attractive Keyes, cute Foch, a flirty hat check girl, and a vivacious Drew. Direction by Robert Rossen is taut but it's the dialogue in the script (also provided by Rossen) that sparkles particularly in Johnny's exchanges with all the women in his life but mostly his moments with Keyes. As for the mystery, the motivations of the murderer aren't quite clear but it works nevertheless. The one main drawback is that the film lacks the kind of atmosphere such movies as *The Big Sleep* or *Maltese Falcon* oozed which may or may not have been the fault of cinematographer Burnett Guffey because the story itself is rather straightforward with few spikes of tension or action. Solid.

Cinematographer Burnett Guffey does have his moments such as this suspenseful scene in *Johnny O'Clock*

Johnny O'Clock had an embaressment of riches: Ellen Drew played Nelle March

Nina Foch played Harriet Hobs

Fear in the Night (1947)

Slight but interesting early noir that really, is more notable for being the film debut of future *Star Trek* regular DeForest Kelley as nondescript bank teller Vince Greyson who wakes up one night after dreaming that he killed a man. Only it's not a dream as a button and key he finds in his coat pocket prove. He confides in brother-in-law Cliff Herlihy (Paul Kelly), a police detective, who of course, doesn't believe a word of it. Events proceed as you'd expect until a Sunday picnic rain storm forces Vince and girlfriend Betty Winters (Kay Scott) along with sister Lil (Ann Doran) and Cliff into a deserted house which so happens to be the scene of the killing Vince had dreamed about! Seems Vince has led them there because of subconscious memories. Now Cliff is angry, thinking that he's been played for a sap by Vince and his inner cop comes out as he begins to give his own brother-in-law the third degree! Hoo boy! Anyway, with more details provided by the slap happy Vince, Cliff figures it all out and nearly gets Vince killed in an attempt to corner the real killer. So so directing by Maxwell Shane keeps things moving and the viewer guessing. Otherwise, nothing much else to report here.

Director Maxwell Shane makes a valiant effort to do something interesting in the otherwise so so *Fear in the Night*. Here, Vince Greyson (DeForest Kelly) tours the death house seen in his dreams

Ann Doran as sister Lil helps dress up the otherwise unremarkable *Fear in the Night*

Our cast: Betty Winters (Kay Scott), Lil (Ann Doran), Vince Greyson (DeForest Kelly), and Cliff Herlihy (Paul Kelly) as Vince wonders about the familiarity of the murder scene they just happened to find while picinicing!

They Live By Night (1948)

First pairing of the Farley Granger and Cathy O'Donnell team is a justified classic of the noir genre. A short intro sets up the two leads Bowie Bowers (played by Granger) and Keechie Mobley (O'Donnell): young people who, through circumstances of birth (both came from broken homes connected to criminal activity) have little knowledge of every day life taken for granted by most normal people. Thus, when they're suddenly thrown together after Bowie and a couple of other escaped convicts take shelter at a run down garage, they discover an attraction for each other. But because they've had no experience in the more tender emotions, Bowie and Keechie are unsure of their feelings. Finally, they decide to run off together. Bowie to escape from his two partners who insist on dragging him into a life of crime and Keechie to get away from a parent she doesn't love. While on the run, spending freely the money stolen during Bowie's last bank job, their awkward relationship grows until they marry at a roadside justice of the peace. At first, the decision to wed seems to be perfunctory but soon enough genuine love grows and pregnancy follows. But just as their happiness becomes complete, Bowie's past catches up to him when his ex-partners appear demanding he rejoin them in another robbery. The irony is that by this time, Bowie has been built up by the media as the dangerous leader of the gang, responsible for any number of murders. And so, when the bank job falls through, Bowie becomes public enemy number one and the object of a nationwide manhunt. He manages to avoid the police but in the end is betrayed and the law guns him down outside the motel room where Keechie is waiting for him. In this film, Bowie's noir decision point takes place off camera, before the story properly begins. That decision is to join fellow ex-cons T-Dub (J.C. Flippen) and Chicamaw Mobley (Howard Da Silva) in escaping from prison. After that, everything is downhill despite the brief happiness Bowie finds in Keechie's love. Direction by Nicholas Ray is flawless as he keeps the camera moving, including revolutionary aerial shots that seem like the eye of God looking down as the characters go through their paces. Ray also took a hand in the script along with Charles Schnee and together, they manage to balance a convincing love story with the darker elements of film noir. A groundbreaking transition film that leapfrogs from the straight crime genre over proto noir to noir proper.

One of director Nicholas Rey's God-like aerial shots looking down on escaping criminals T-Dub, Chicamaw Mobley. and Bowie Bowers

On the lam: T. Dub (J.C. Flippen), Bowie Bower (Farley Granger), and Chicamaw Mobley (Howard Da Silva)

Kathy O'Donnell's girl next door looks made her perfect for the role of the naive Keechie Mobley

Brute Force (1947)

A jail break picture to end all jail break pictures, *Brute Force* is cold and hard with no room for sentimentality. And when sentimentality does try to raise its head, it's immediately slapped down, overridden by a sense of hopelessness as a group of jailbirds plot an escape from prison. But everything about the film including its harsh cinematography by William Daniels signals to the viewer, as it should have to the inmates, that escape was impossible. But tell that to Joe Collins (played by Burt Lancaster) who nurses resentment for hated prison captain Munsey (Hume Cronyn) and is desperate to break out so that he can keep his promise to ailing girlfriend Ruth (Ann Blyth) that he would return to her, a promise even he knows on a subconscious level can never be fulfilled. But learning that Ruth refuses to have her illness treated unless he is with her, he presses on. Recruiting cellmates Stack (Jeff Corey), Spencer (John Hoyt), Robert Becker (Howard Duff), and Tom Lister (Whit Bissell), he plans to escape while the group is on a press gang outside the walls. Well, the day of the break comes and as expected, everything goes wrong. The prison doctor played by Art Smith has the last word: "Nobody escapes, nobody really escapes." But did he mean from prison or from memories of the outside that haunt the would be escapees? Although the film suffers some from an excessive use of sets over actual locations, director Jules Dassin does a good job in making viewers forget all that as he puts his characters through their paces aided in no small part by Cronyn whose sadistic ways keep the inmates on edge. Cronyn is especially menacing during an interrogation scene. As the prisoner is tied to a chair in his office, he calmly continues to rinse his hands before picking up a rubber hose... Lancaster is intense and barely cracks a smile through the whole picture but then, he doesn't have much to be happy about...except those moments when stool pigeons are given their just desserts including one killed after being crushed in an industrial press and another shot to death while tied to the front of a rail car and used as a human shield. Whew! In all, the cast is a name droppers dream and all play their parts to perfection in this blackest of film noirs.

A sorry group of jailbirds: Robert Becker (Howard Duff), Spencer (John Hoyt), Tom Lister (Whit Bissell), Stack (Jeff Corey), and, Joe Collins (Burt Lancaster)

Ann Blyth: What drove Joe Collins' hopeless escape attempt!

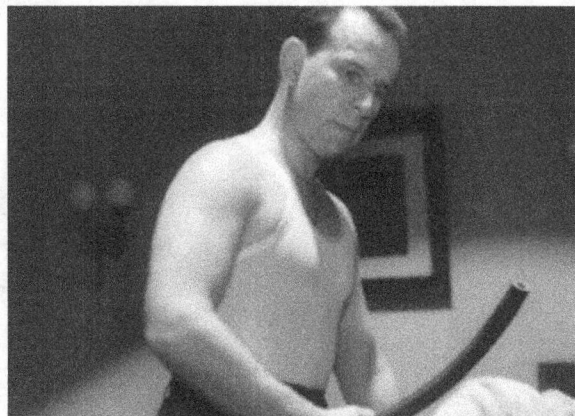

Hume Cronyn put in a command performance with his portrayal of the sadistic Capt. Munsey

Possessed (1947)

It's role reversal time as Louise Howell (Joan Crawford) falls hard for engineer David Sutton (Van Heflin). (In film noir, it's usually the guy who falls for the femme fatale) But David has no use for Louise and calls off their relationship. This sets off Louise who becomes obsessed with David even claiming that by marrying her rich employer (for whom she works as private nurse for his ailing wife) her intention was to make David jealous. Yeah, right! The plot begins at the end when we see a mind blasted Louise wandering the streets of Washington DC asking strangers about David. She winds up in a psych ward where under drugs, she spills the beans to a kindly doctor. Now the viewer learns the full story of how Louise slowly descended into madness. While continuing to obsess about David, she begins to hallucinate (one of the best scenes in the movie involves a whole sequence that ends with Louise pushing her step daughter down a flight of stairs only to have it revealed that it was just her imagination) and to suffer from a guilt complex. She finally snaps after learning that David intends to marry step daughter Carol (Geraldine Brooks). Confronting David at last, she ends up shooting him in a scene that actually takes viewers by surprise. That's where she ends up wandering the mean streets of Washington. A longish film, *Possessed* is well directed by Curtis Burnhardt who was influenced by the early German filmmakers. (His opening scenes as Louise is brought to the psych ward are inventive as are many other sequences in the film) Burnhardt is abetted with great cinematography by Joseph Valentine who literally paints in shadow and light creating a constant atmosphere of paranoia. Sort of a combination woman's film and film noir, *Possessed* satisfies on a number of levels. Crawford, never a very attractive actress, fits the part here because the viewer can believe it when David dumps her and husband to be Raymond Massey as Dean Graham catches her on the rebound. With her arch, bug eyed look, Crawford easily convinces as a woman descending into madness. A girlishly attractive Geraldine Brooks as Carol Graham is her opposite, convincing in the role of the ingenue that threatens Louise' fantasy about getting back with David. Raymond Massey is miscast unless it was the intention that he be a cold, removed husband who can't make anyone believe he actually loves Louise!

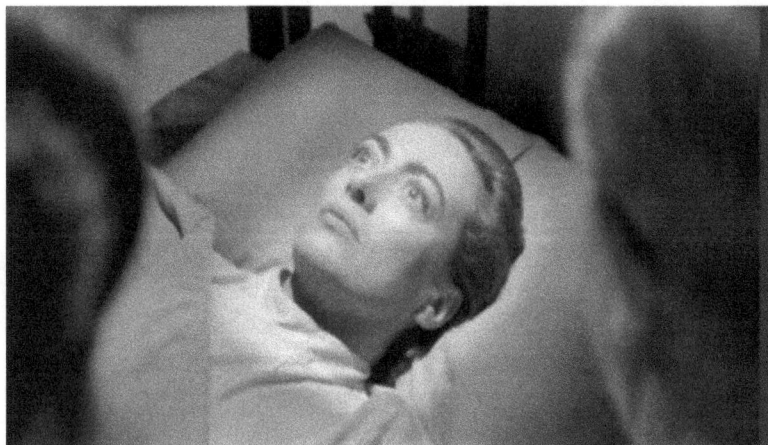

An insane Louise Howell (Joan Crawford) falls into a catatonic state following her shooting of imagined lover David Sutton

It's plain that a youthful Geraldine Brooks could drive an older woman insane with jealousy!

The kiss off: David Sutton (Van Heflin) gives Louise Howell (Joan Crawford) the bad news. He doesn't love her.

Desperate (1947)

Hapless trucker Steve Randall (played by noir regular Steve Brodie) is suckered into taking part in a warehouse robbery. Not liking the idea, he manages to signal a passing beat cop that something's up. Result: the cop is killed by the brother of mob boss Walt Radak (Raymond Burr). Now, an angry Radak wants to pin the murder on Randall and set his brother free. He has Randall beaten but he refuses to cooperate. Next, his young wife Anne (Audrey Long) is threatened. That does it. The couple pack up and hit the road with the intention of hiding out on a farm belonging to Anne's relatives. Meanwhile, the cops catch up to Radak and he's wounded in a gunfight. Recovering, he's madder than ever, hires a crooked PI to locate Randall and then heads out to the farm. When he gets there, it's too late to save his brother who's scheduled to die in the electric chair at midnight so he plans to kill Randall at the exact same moment! Adding to poor Randall's complications is the fact that Anne is pregnant and his refusal to go to the police for help. Sure, the police were looking for him in connection with the cop's murder but mostly this lack of judgment was just a means of prolonging the plot. Still, you can't get more economical than a film that clocks in at just 83 minutes and director Anthony Mann uses every one of those minutes to drive his story forward (while allowing some confusion in timing and geography along the way). A so-so film as noir, but nonetheless interesting for all that.

Steve Randall (Steve Brodie) and Walt Radak (Raymond Burr) face off at the climax of *Desperate* as the clock ticks toward midnight...

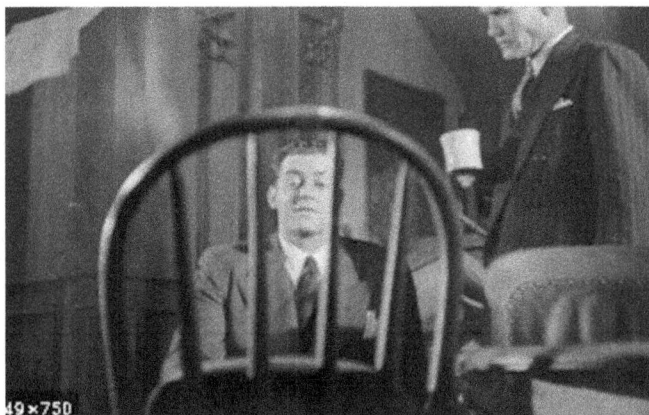

Director Anthony Mann uses this clever shot to illustrate the fate of Radak's brother, due to be executed for murder, and perhaps that of Radak himself should be be found by the police

In happier times: Steve and Anne Randall look forward to a new arrival

Ride the Pink Horse (1947)

Somewhat overlong proto-noir sees Robert Montgomery directing and starring as ex-veteran and small time hood Lucky Gagin in possession of a canceled check that proves big time mob figure Frank Hugo (Fred Clark) cheated the government during the war. Gagin travels to San Pablo, a small New Mexican town that seems no different than any other town in Mexico proper seeking to blackmail Hugo. In no time, he falls prey to a number of Hugo's henchman as well as femme fatale Marjorie Lundeen (Andrea King). Beat up and stabbed, Gagin ends up frustrating Hugo by simply handing the evidence to government man Bill Retz (Art Smith). In between all that is where the film drags somewhat as Gagin falls in with the local Mexican-American community and is befriended by a teenager named Pila (Wanda Hendrix). He more or less dismisses her out of hand but as things turn out, ends up needing her help in order to stay alive. Also in the cast is merry go round operator Pancho (Thomas Gomez) who not only provides him a bed for the night but takes a beating for him in one of the film's most chilling scenes where Pancho is given a going over by a couple of Hugo's goons as the merry go round operates in the foreground and the kids on it growing more and more upset at the cruelty being perpetrated just behind them. In good noir style, audience expectations are dashed when Gagin turns his back on Pila and leaves her where he found her. All she has for her experience are stories with which to regale her friends. Cinematography by Russell Metty is atmospheric despite scenes being shot mostly on soundstages. The script by Ben Hecht and Charles Lederer adapting the novel by Dorothy Hughes is tight as likewise is Montgomery's direction with the standout scene being Gagin's arrival in San Pablo and his hiding the evidence at a bus station done all in a single take. Montgomery's portrayal of Gagin as emotionless and naively self confident is intriguing and conforms with the noir motif of a veteran returning from war and finding nothing for him in a peacetime USA. *Pink Pony* is a different kind of underworld noir that's nevertheless worthy of the afficionado's attention.

Where many a film noir begin: Lucky Gagin arrives in town and trouble soon follows

Dangerous: Marjorie Lundeen (Andrea King)

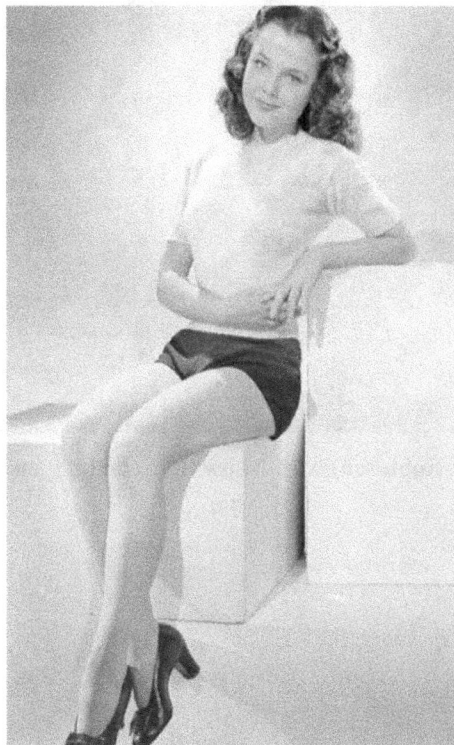

Wanda Hendrix played the endearing Mexican teen Pila but she failed to ingratiate herself on the unsentimental Lucky Gagin

Key Largo (1948)

So so noir with a claustrophobic effect due to most of the scenes taking place indoors and use of interior/exterior sets which become particularly obvious when the camera faces out to sea (actually a gigantic water tank on the Warners lot) showing a model of a cabin cruiser on the horizon. That said, the effect is excellent especially when Indians in row boats are seen in the foreground. The script by Richard Brooks and John Huston (who also directed) is based on a play with a much darker spin than the happy ending the movie gives viewers. Humphrey Bogart plays Frank McCloud, an Army veteran come to the isolated hotel on Key Largo to give owner James Temple (Lionel Barrymore) a first hand account of his son's death in combat. But instead, he stumbles onto a hostage situation wherein wanted mobster Johnny Rocco (Edward G. Robinson) and his gang is hiding out. What follows is a battle of wits between Frank and Johnny. In between, Frank falls in love with Nora Temple (Lauren Bacall) and is seemingly exposed as a coward. In reality, he's just world weary because in the end, he comes through and saves the day in a long awaited but thrilling climax. A good cast and direction by Huston however, can't save this rather slow story that only touches on the edges of film noir. Instead, one might see this as an epilogue to Hollywood's earlier romance with the gangster genre. If Johnny Rocco can be considered representative of such mob precursors as Little Ceasar, then *Key Largo* gives a hint at how they became anachronisms in the post war era.

Johnny Rocco (Edward G. Robinson) with fellow thugs looking on, counts the loot from his latest job

Nora Temple (Lauren Bacall) looks on as Frank McCloud (Humphrey Bogart}
explains his philosophy of life

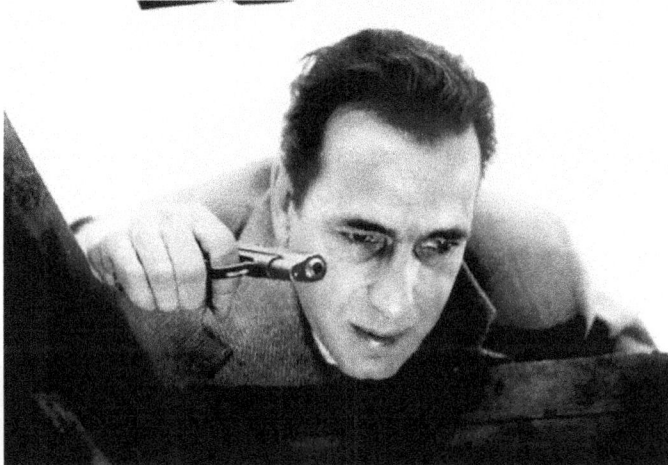

Frank McCloud waits for Johnny Rocco to emerge from the boat's
cabin at the long in coming climax to *Key Largo*

Force of Evil (1948)

In a case of if you play in mud you're going to get muddy, attorney Joe Morse (John Garfield) has allowed himself first to defend mob boss Ben Tucker in court, then to become his partner in the numbers running racket. Now, Tucker has a plan to fix the Fourth of July game so that it will bankrupt all the independent operators in the city forcing them to come to him for loans after which, he'll own them lock, stock, and barrel. Only problem for Joe though, is that the brother he owes his legal career to is one of those small timers. Even worse, Leo Morse (Thomas Gomez) styles himself an honest man and would rather go bankrupt than be taken over by Tucker. But due to Leo's bad heart, bankruptcy could kill him. Not to worry, Joe has a plan: fix it so that Leo can go to work for Tucker and make easy money. But Leo rebels, putting him on a collision course with two warring underworld factions. Complicating things for Joe is the fact that he's fallen in love with Leo's cute secretary Doris Lowry (Beatrice Pearson). Anyway, things go south for Joe as Leo is kidnapped and dies while in the hands of rival mobster Bill Ficco (Paul Fix) with the final scene of the film a moving climax to the wages of Joe's sins. Directed by Abraham Polonsky (who he?) the movie has an hypnotic drive as it opens with Joe already caught in the coils of crime and heading to his dark rendezvous with noir destiny. The film also doesn't stint in its depiction of mob behavior with crooked cops and innocents unable to escape from the quicksand of criminal enterprise. Both Garfield and Gomez fit their roles while the gangsters are rather non-descript (with noir regular Marie Windsor cheap as Tucker's wife). The standout though is newcomer Pearson whose innocence and fresh faced appearance steals the show especially in a long scene as she and Garfield share a taxi ride.

Climactic scene in *Force of Evil* as Joe Morse (John Garfield) proceeds to his inevitable noir destiny

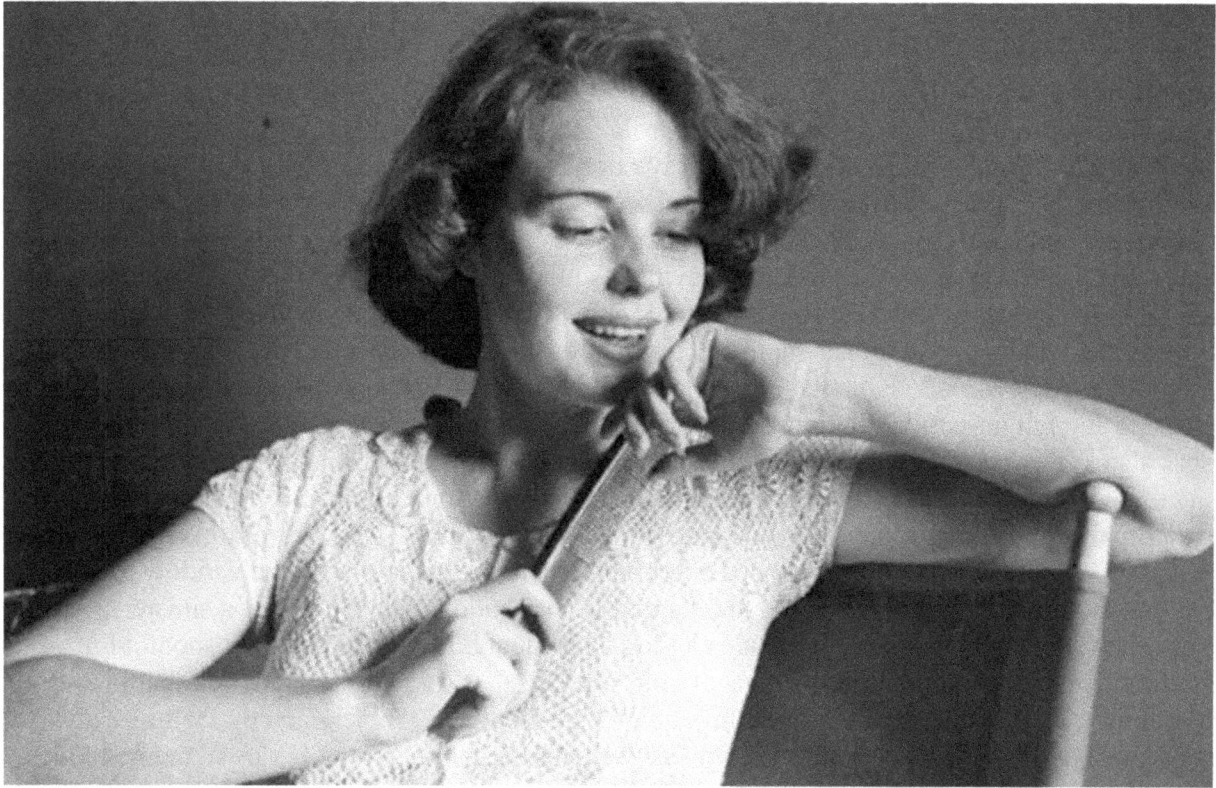

Beatrice Pearson, as Doris Lowry, entered the picture too late to save Joe Morse from his fate

Tawdry Marie Windsor, as Edna Tucker, tries and fails to seduce Joe Morse intro betraying her mob boss husband and take up with her

Raw Deal (1948)

The film opens the way many noirs do: with a prison escape. Jailbird Joe Sullivan (Dennis O'Keefe) is impatient. He can't wait the three years to make parole. He needs to "breathe fresh air" and collect the $50,000 owed him by gang leader Rick Coyle (Raymond Burr) for taking the fall for a crime that's never explained. With the help of love sick Pat Regan (Claire Trevor), Joe breaks out of jail and after switching cars a number of times, ends up at the apartment of sympathetic case worker Ann Martin (Marsha Hunt). Forced by the police to keep moving, Joe kidnaps Ann and the threesom form an odd romantic triangle. It doesn't help that Ann is better looking than Pat and soon develops Stockholm syndrome as she falls in love with her captor. Their relationship climaxes so to speak, after Ann saves Joe by shooting Coyle torpedo Fantail (John Ireland). After that, no one in the audience is surprised when she and Joe fall into each other's arms out there on the moonlit beach! But this is film noir and so audiences also knew it couldn't end well. It doesn't. But the joy of *Raw Deal* is in the getting there and doing a great job helping things along the predictable path is director Anthony Mann aided by cinematographer John Alton. Mann sets things up by making sure almost the entire film takes place at night with key scenes such as Ann's darkened apartment where Joe creeps in by the window to snatch her from dreamland; the fight between Joe and Fantail in the shadowy back room of a sinister taxidermy shop; the fog bound streets outside Coyle's apartment building; or the final shootout in Coyle's apartment. All made to order for fans of noir. And let's not forget the soundtrack that includes the unusual use of a theramin granting the film's quieter moments a genuinely creepy feeling. Those interludes come as background to Pat's narration as she tells Joe's story and of her own doomed love. Excellent all around for a poverty row effort with top notch casting in O'Keefe, Hunt, Trevor (just attractive enough to hold a mug's interest...until someone like Hunt comes along), Ireland, and Burr (if his bad guy status needed any convincing, throwing the flaming contents of his baked Alaska into his girlfriend's face ought to do it). Don't miss this one noir fans!

Anthony Mann, the man behind many of the era's most memorable noirs

Marsha Hunt

Cool shot from Raw Deal

Hollow Triumph (1948)

Sometimes listed under the title "The Scar," *Hollow Triumph* follows the classic noir pattern with the slight variation in that instead of an innocent who makes a wrong decision and spirals down to his just desserts, the protagonist here isn't so innocent. But that little thing doesn't stop this film from being good. In fact, it's not bad at all despite having the wooden Paul Henreid in the lead. You see, Henreid plays ex-con John Muller who is released from prison with no intention of going straight. Getting his old gang back together again, he overrides their concerns and robs a mob gambling casino. Big mistake. While the rest of his gang are killed off, Muller goes underground taking various low rung jobs to escape notice. That is, until he discovers his double in the form of psychiatrist Dr. Victor Bartok. Changing his looks to increase the resemblance between himself and the good doctor (including adding a scar to his cheek...on the wrong side!), he murders the doctor and takes his place. Along the way, he falls in love with Bartok's secretary, the obviously conflicted Evelyn Hahn (Joan Bennett) which complicates matters. Anyway, Muller succeeds in evading the mob hit men only to be cornered at the last minute in an ironic twist. Suffice it to say, it all ends in classic noir style as Muller gets what's coming to him. Produced by Henreid and ostensibly directed by Steve Sekely (Henreid eventually replaced him at the insistence of the studio) the film keeps the viewer's interest right from the start as you wonder what's going to happen next. Henreid is okay in the role of Muller (despite a slight accent) and Joan Bennett is luminous as usual. Good one.

John Muller (Paul Henreid) fingers the scar on his face as Evelyn Hahn (Joan Bennett) looks on. Does she notice that the scar is on the wrong side of her boss' face

Marcy (Herbert Rudley) tries to talk John Muller into going straight after being released from prison. No such luck.

Joan Bennett: John Muller gave all this up for murder and the wages of crime? But such witless decisions are what noir is all about!

He Walked By Night (1948)

Police procedural based on an actual case of a clever cop killer and disturbed World War II veteran who manages to stay one step ahead of the law until finally captured. In the movie, however, events are inverted to heighten the drama. In real life, Erwin Walker went on his crime spree before killing a policeman. For the film, the action opens with Roy Martin's (Richard Basehart) murder of a policeman before going on a crime spree ending with a chase through the LA sewer system and being shot dead by pursuing cops. There's much hay made of the fact that the sewer chase predated a similar sequence in *The Third Man*, but really, this film doesn't come up to that level of quality. Made on the cheap, it nevertheless rises above its lowly origins due mainly to two factors: Basehart's restrained performance as Martin and cinematography by John Alton. Eschewing the use of overhead lighting that would have left everything over lit, Alton instead, lights most scenes from below or indirectly. The results are stunning as characters move in a shrouded, night time world of shadows and darkness. The film also boasts appearances by a couple of mainstays from SF cinema including a lengthy role for Whit Bissell as the mousy and perhaps corrupt businessman Paul Reeves and the great Kenneth Tobey (star of *The Thing*) in a tiny, uncredited role as a detective. Solid.

Police search for the fugitive Roy Martin in the city sewers. Cinematography by John Alton. Notice the wires trailing from the flashlights. It was the only way Alton could get enough power to light the darkened tunnels and make the shot work.

More Alton magic as Roy Martin (Richard Basehart) cases his next job

After starring in a number of classic film noirs, Richard Basehart became a genre mainstay

Pitfall (1948)

Insurance salesman John Forbes (Dick Powell) suffers a mid-life crisis when he falls for blond bombshell Mona Stevens (noir queen Lizabeth Scott) in this film that sticks pretty close to what would soon enough become a film noir trope. Namely, ordinary guy makes one wrong move and it ruins his life. In this case, Forbes is assigned to recover items from Mona that were purchased with her boyfriend's ill gotten gains. Said boyfriend now safely jailed, Forbes finds himself forgetting his average middle class life with wife Sue (Jane Wyatt) and son Tommy (Jimmy Hunt) for Mona's charms. Compounding his troubles is PI Mac MacDonald (Raymond Burr), who's already stuck on Mona and doesn't value the competition. Following him home one night (after the film suggests that Forbes had committed adultery with Mona) Mac warns him off by way of a beating. For a time, Forbes stays away from Mona but when she calls to say Mac is stalking her, he again makes the wrong decision and becomes involved. This time, Mac goes to Mona's jailbird boyfriend and puts a bug in his ear. When he's released, the boyfriend comes after Forbes who ends up shooting him. Now he's betrayed his family and killed a man to boot! But it's not over yet but to say any more would be telling! Suffice it to say, *Pitfall* is a classic noir set up and worth seeing by any fan!

John Forbes (Dick Powell) risks a wonderful home life including wife Sue (Jane Wyatt) to fool around with jailbait Mona Stevens

John Forbes faced a big decision: Jane Wyatt...

...or Lizabeth Scott

Set-Up (1949)

With its brutally realistic depiction of the fight game and the personality types that haunt its arenas, *The Set-Up* is quite likely the best boxing movie ever! Masterfully directed by Robert Wise in close to real time, the film stars Robert Ryan (as Stoker Thompson), an old warhorse on his last legs still dreaming of one last victory in the squared circle. But long suffering wife Julie (Audrey Totter) knows better deciding to stay away and not attend the match as she has every one before. While she wanders through the sleezy underbelly of society in the neighborhood of the arena, pondering her husband's fate, Stoker is in the crowded locker room psyching himself up for the match while checking hopefully out the window for evidence that Julie will be in the audience. A parade of contenders move in and out of the dingy locker room each wrestling with their own demons whether of confidence or delusion or simple madness. Finally, it's Stoker's turn to meet the much younger Tiger Nelson (Hal Fieberling) in scenes shot by Wise (with harsh cinematography by Milton Krasner) that are uncompromising in their realism. But as the viewer roots for Stoker, unbeknownst by him, he's been sold out by his unscrupulous manager (George Tobias). Unwilling to ask Stoker to take a dive, Tiny has taken money from a local gangster named Little Boy (Alan Baxter) in the belief that the washed up Stoker will lose to the younger Nelson anyway. Wrong! When Stoker manages to slog through four rounds of headbashing fury to victory, Tiny takes a powder leaving Stoker to face the music. Based on a poem by Joseph March and significantly altered, the film was vastly superior with Ryan the perfect casting not only for his haggard looks and acting ability but due to the fact that he'd been a heavyweight boxer himself in real life. Despite her reputation as a femme fatale, Audrey Totter fitted surprisingly well as the sympathetic Julie and George Tobias emerges from his usual comic sidekick role to fit the bill as Stoker's hapless manager. Supporting players seen mostly in locker room scenes included noir regular James Edwards, Dobie Gillis' real life big brother Darryl Hickman, and later silver screen regular Philip Pine, all playing boxers of different stripes. Shot mostly on a backlot, Wise captures the other side of the tracks feel of drunks, prostitutes, and petty thugs that inhabit the area around the arena and a tracking shot of Julie as she walks past barkers and strip joints to a bridge overlooking oncoming trains underscores her mood of personal desolation. The story itself is shot in real time with an opening shot of a street clock showing the time as 9:05 p.m. and an identical shot at the end showing the same clock at 10:16. Very close to the film's actual 72 minute running time. The four rounds of battle between Stoker and Tiger seems much longer than it really is and was shot by Wise using three cameras for close ups, wide angle shots, and pick ups that combine to create the illusion of a real slugfest. Any way you look at it, this film is totally excellent!

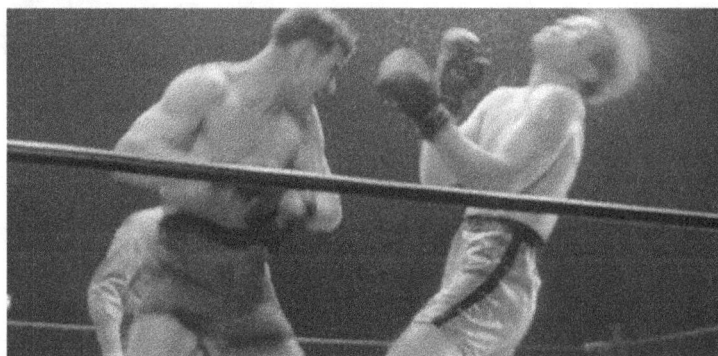

Stoker's fight with Tiger Nelson was pure bone jarring realism

Ominous scene at the climax to *The Set-Up* as Stoker gets set to take on mobsters intent on giving him the works for failing to throw the fight

Julie Thompson (Audrey Totter) agonizes over the fate of her aging husband as he battles in the arena across the street

The Big Steal (1949)

The teaming of Robert Mitchum and Jane Greer worked so well on *Out of the Past*, the studio decided to bring them back together again for *The Big Steal*. And though Greer is attractive, she lost much of her glamor in between films. In a plot that would resemble the following year's *Borderline*, Mitchum (as Lt. Duke Halliday) and Greer (as Joan Graham) end up in a chase across Mexico. At first reluctant partners, they of course, fall in love by the finish. In between, the viewer learns that Halliday is being chased by Capt. Vincent Blake (William Bendix) ostensibly to recover an Army payroll that Halliday is blamed for stealing. And although the viewer is kept in suspense as to whether or not that was true there was very little doubt that Halliday wasn't a crook. (Mitchum had been arrested for the possession of marijuana shortly before the movie was made so there was a veneer of criminality about him even so) In the meantime, Joan has been jilted by fiance, Jim Fiske (Patric Knowles) who actually has the money. Now Joan is after him to repay money he owes her thus, she's unwilling to remain behind as Halliday races to recover the payroll. Suffice it to say, the conclusion provides a number of surprises and the expected happy ending. Don Siegel's direction is fast paced with a script by a trio of writers who, among them, manage to provide Mitchum and Greer with plenty of witty dialogue and snarky comebacks. Filmed entirely in Mexico, the film is backstopped with plenty of genuine atmosphere.

Vincent Blake (William Bendix) gets the drop on Duke Halliday (Robert Mitchum) early in *The Big Steal*

Perhaps not as luminously beautiful as she was in *Out of the Past,* Jane Greer nevertheless, had the goods!

Duke Halliday (Robert Mitchum) and Joan Graham (Jane Greer) spent much of *The Big Steal* driving around and trading quips...when they weren't being ambushed or giving Vncent Blake (William Bendix) the slip.

Act of Violence (1949)

Frank Enley's (played by Van Heflin) big mistake took place before the moody opening shots of *Act of Violence*. As an Air Force pilot captured by the Nazis and placed in a POW camp, Enley had sold out the rest of his crew for a crust of bread. In doing so, he inadvertantly condemned them to death. All except one, former best friend Joe Parkson (Robert Ryan). With his lame leg, Parkson survived and began hunting down Enley in order to kill him. That's where the opening scenes of *Act of Violence* take up the story. Parkson follows Enley to California where Enley is married to wife Edith (Janet Leigh) and has become a successful, well liked citizen of Santa Lisa. After a series of near meetings, a panicky Enley flees into the night. Meanwhile, Parkson's wife (Phyllis Thaxter) also appears on the scene to beg Parkson to abandon his quest to kill Enley. Drunk and despondent, Enley is scraped off the street by barfly Pat (a tired looking Mary Astor) who takes him to a sleazy underworld attorney who tells him he can fix his problem if the money is right. Though, Enley recoils at the suggestion of murder, the attorney refuses to give up on such an easy mark and sends hitman Johnny (Berry Kroeger) after him. After learning Parkson's whereabout, Kroeger proceeds to set up a meeting in order to kill him but Enley beats him to the rendezvous and catches the bullet meant for Parkson. In a final, desperate attempt to save Parkson and perhaps make amends, Enley causes Kroeger to crash his getaway car and is killed in the process. A fitting, noirish end for a weak willed joe who took the wrong road somewhere in his past. After a really great, atmospheric opening in early morning misty Los Angeles photographed by Robert Surtees, the action of the film shifts to sunny Santa Lisa and then location work at Big Bear Lake. Director Fred Zinnemann then takes the viewer back to the Enley's home where Surtees goes to town with shadowy, darkened interiors as Enley's world suddenly squeezes him into a tight, psychological corner. Liquor joints, backroom dives, and Pat's seamy apartment are all suitably grimy looking. Ryan is good as a human time bomb just as Johnson could always be counted on as the hapless regular joe. The film is unusual for having three strong female leads including Leigh as the worried wife, Thaxter as the woman determined to save her man from making a big mistake, and Astor as the floozy and possible prostitute that falls in with Enley. As noir as they come.

Location shooting such as this, as Frank Enley flees in panic, really opened up *Act of Violence* creating a mood of desperation and ever shrinking opportunities for escape from the noir dilemma

Hard to believe that casting directors for *Act of Violence* saw a typical housewife in Janet Leigh!

The climax to *Act of Violence:* Frank Enley takes one for Joe Parkson

D.O.A. (1949)

One of the true classics of the genre, *D.O.A.* provides a star turn for noir regular Edmund O'Brien as Frank Bigelow, an accountant who makes the mistake of notarizing a bill of sale that someone is eager to keep out of the public eye. Eager enough to kill him over it. Unlike the typical noir set up where an ordinary guy makes the wrong decision and ends up suffering the consequences, here, the hapless protagonist does something without the knowledge that it could prove detrimental to him. Thus, while on a trip to San Francisco to get away from Paula Gibson, his cloying secretary (Pamela Britton), Bigelow is poisoned by parties unknown. When doctors tell him that he has only days to live, like most normal people, he refuses to believe them but quickly enough as his condition worsens, he comes around and becomes determined to find his own killer before he keels over for good. What follows is one of the most breathless, frenetic searches in all of filmdom. Director Rudolph Mate tracks Bigelow from clue to clue as he strong arms pretty secretaries, muscles in on grieving widows, and falls afoul of the local crime lord. All the while coming to terms with the fact that while his own life winds down, he realizes the importance of his love for Paula. The screenplay by Russell Rouse and Clarence Greene is airtight with the single out of place element provided by the trill of a kazoo every time the skirt chasing Bigelow eyes a woman...and he eyes *every* woman! While seemingly out of place in such a dead serious film, when the trilling ends after Bigelow's diagnosis and his true feelings for Paula emerge, its absence becomes almost symbolic. But before the trilling disappears completely, Bigelow is still in cherche la femme mode and in fact, it's while cozying up to one of those women at a jazz bar that his killer switches his drink for one doused with luminous toxin, the poison that finally does him in. Location shooting in 'Frisco helps the film immeasurably with shots of Market Street, the Fisherman Club, and the Bradbury Building all prominent. In fact, the credits open with Bigelow mounting the steps of the police department seeking the homicide bureau. In one of the most innovative openings of any noir, he steps into the lieutenant's office and declares that he wants to report a murder. Who's murder, asks the police lieutenant. Mine, states Bigelow before telling his story. At which point, the film flashes back to the events leading up to the dramatic opening. The film ends where it began but with Bigelow falling over dead. The last word on his lips the name of his secretary: Paula. That's when the movie receives its title as the lieutenant tells the others in the room to list Bigelow as "Dead on arrival!"

Frank Bigelow (Edmund O'Brien) in one of the many scrapes he falls into while seeking his killer

Pamela Britton played cloying secretary Paula Gibson

Establishing shot from *DOA* features the well known Fisherman night club and other 'Frisco landmarks

Border Incident (1949)

As timely today as it was back in 1949, *Border Incident* features behind the scenes, procedural elements of federal agencies at work trying to uncover an illegal alien smuggling ring operating across the border with Mexico. Headed by big agri businessman Owen Parkson (played by smoothly sinister Howard Da Silva), the operation is a cooperative effort between Americans and Mexican criminals who smuggle workers across the border to work on farms for low wages only to rob and/or kill them once they return to Mexico. To break the ring, the American government assigns Jack Bearns (George Murphy) to go undercover with traceable work permits for sale. He's aided by Pablo Rodriguez (Ricardo Montalban), a Mexican fed who infiltrates the smuggling network as a migrant worker. But just as the trap is sprung, Bearns is discovered and killed in one of the most harrowing scenes in the proto-noir period: shot and clubbed in a field, he's run over by a tractor hauling a multi-bladed harrow while Rodriguez looks on helplessly. For this sequence, director Anthony Mann chose to drop any ambient music and even Bearns' screams of terror with only the sound of the approaching tractor grinding into the viewer's mind. At a low angle, from Bearns' POV, the camera captures the oncoming tractor as it looms larger and larger until it seems to fill the entire world before cutting back to Rodriguez' stunned reaction. As Bearns, Murphy is rather wooden in quieter scenes but comes alive in those involving extreme stress such as when he's captured and tortured by Mexican criminals or after he realizes his cover has been blown. As his Mexican counterpart, Montalban is cool and natural in his dual roles and it's easy to see why he ended up with a long career in Hollywood. Mann himself however, is the real star of the film with tight direction that maintains tension throughout the story culminating in a quicksand scene that's genuinely edge of the seat material. Cinematography by John Alton is superb with most of the film shot at night and on locations that, if not really the back alleys of some Mexican border town, might as well have been. Alton uses shadows and darkness expertly to create a lingering atmosphere of menace that manages to make viewers feel the same level of anxiety as Bearns and Rodriguez as every minute could see them exposed and killed in some horrid manner. Noir fave Charles McGraw is suitably gruff as Parkson's henchman Jeff Amboy, but whoever the woman was who played his wife really takes the cake!

Harrowing point of view shot as Jack Bearns (George Murphy) waits to be run over by a tractor

Mexican federal agent Pablo Rodriguez (Ricardo Montalban) infiltrates the human smuggling operation

Cinematographer John Alton's use of key lighting here serves to accentuate and symbolize Owen Parkson's (Howard da Silva) evil

Killer Bait (1949)

How can you not love a film noir called *Killer Bait*? Much better than the more dulcet *Too Late For Tears* that this near fogotten gem was labeled upon initial release. That said, *Killer Bait* doesn't exactly match the main action of the film which involves one of the nastiest of bad girls as she goes from ordinary housewife to thief to liar to murderess. And best of all, it ends exactly the way the best film noirs should. Noir favorite Lizabeth Scott as Jane Palmer is the housewife in question and Arthur Kennedy as her milquetoast husband, Alan. The whole thing begins when the Palmers' car is mistaken for another and a bag of money ($60,000) is tossed into the back seat. He wants to turn it over to the police, she wants to keep it. From there, one thing leads to another as the dominoes begin to fall, bigger and bigger dominoes that is! Complicating Jane's greedy ambitions is Danny Fuller (Dan Duryea) as the original thief who wants his money back; Kathy Palmer (Kristine Miller), Alan's nosy sister; and Don "Blake" (Don DeFore) who claims to be a friend of Alan's. Competently directed by Byron Haskin, the film isn't especially noteworthy for atmospheric cinematography nor for location shooting (although there is some from around Los Angeles), but its twisty plot, building suspense, and performances by Scott and Duryea more than make up for it.

Don "Blake" (Don DeFore) and Kathy Palmer (Kristine Miller) get more than they bargained for when they decide to drop in on Jane Palmer (Lizabeth Scott) to ask the whereabouts of her missing husband

Milquetoast husband Alan Palmer (Arthur Kennedy) arrives home only to find that wife Jane is already eager to spend the stolen loot

Lemme fatale Lizabeth Scott could turn on the heat

The Killer That Stalked New York (1950)

Sort of a combination film noir and medical thriller, this film throws the viewer directly into the action and never lets go. It follows two stories in parallel as Federal investigators look for diamond smugglers and a team of doctors and city officials try to find patient zero who is spreading smallpox across New York. Their target is the same: Sheila Bennet (Evelyn Keyes) who arrives in town from Cuba sick and looking for husband Matt (Charles Korvin). But Matt is a creep. While she was away getting the diamonds, he was fooling around with her better looking sister, Francie (Lola Albright). He plans to run away with the sister and the diamonds leaving Sheila in the lurch. But even as Sheila stumbles around town looking for Matt and aiming to gun him down, people begin to die from the smallpox she's carrying including Francie. Director Earl McEvoy does a good job balancing the two investigations and keeping viewer interest high while cinematographer Joseph Biroc does noir proud, particularly in the scene where Sheila finally corners Matt. Of interest is that this film has not one, but two bad girls: Sheila and Francie, and one good girl, Dorothy Malone as the loyal and courageous nurse helping to tackle the smallpox epidemic. She's supported by William Bishop as the stoic but guilt ridden doctor who let the sick Sheila slip between his fingers. The film is helped immeasurably by being shot almost entirely on location in New York City and becomes more timely than ever in the wake of the recent corona virus scare. Efforts taken by the city to stem the smallpox epidemic are all eerily familiar with the same concerns, the same catch phrases, the same action taken. Speeches given to explain the danger to the viewer could have been used again to explain the spread of the corona virus. A solid little film that has become more timely than ever.

Location shooting does wonders for *The Killer That Stalked New York* as Sheila Bennet (Evelyn Keyes) waits for the train while searching for her no good husband

Lola Albright played cheating sister Francie; in noir style, she receives her just desserts

Sheila Bennet (Evelyn Keyes) catches up to no good husband Matt (Charles Korvin)

Backfire (1950)

Still very much in the immediate post-war period, *Backfire* features a common theme for proto-noir of the time: the returned war vet who is somewhat damaged physically or psychologically by his combat experiences or who is having difficulty readjusting to civilian life. There's a little of both here as Bob Corey (played by Gordon MacRea) is in a veterans' hospital recovering from wounds. He's in contact with best friend Steve Connolley (Edmond O'Brien) with whom he plans to buy a ranch upon his release from the hospital. But Connelley disappears and one night, Corey is visited by Lysa Radoff (Viveca Lindfors) who tells him his friend has suffered a bad accident and then is gone. When he gets out of the hospital, police inform Corey that Connelly is wanted for the murder of racketeer Solly Blayne. Renting the same hotel room last used by Connelly, Corey embarks on his own investigation into his friend's disappearance finally ending in a confrontation with the real murderer. *Backfire* falls into the murder mystery category of proto-noir films and the script by Ivan Goff serves its purpose well moving its characters from point to point until finally maneuvering them into the film's concluding sequence. But it wasn't as easy as it sounds! Goff uses a series of flashbacks from the POV of different characters to help tell the back story as Corey's investigation evolves, placing the script in danger of falling into a confusing mess. But Goff and director Vincent Sherman pull it off climaxing in a bizarre scene where Connolly, encased in a body cast and neck brace, tackles the bad guy and saves Corey from being shot! Virginia Mayo provides the eye candy this time as the nurse Corey has fallen in love with and who does a bit of sleuthing herself and Viveca Lindfors, O'Brien's dangerous romantic interest, wasn't bad on the eyes either. Genuine L.A. locations like City Hall and the Fremont Hotel and various area neighborhoods helped the action immensely.

Julie Benson (Virginia Mayo) takes a ride with Ben Arno (Dane Clark): Is he friend or foe?

No wonder Gordon McRae made such a rapid recovery what with Virginia Mayo as his nurse!

As femme fatales go, Viveca Lindfors could fill the bill

Borderline (1950)

Besides being a rare instance of a lighthearted noir, *Borderline* involves a popular Hollywood theme, that of the hot pursuit across Mexico usually by a couple trying to make it to the border before they're caught. This time, however, the twist is that the couple concerned are both members of the law enforcement community (she's an L.A. policewoman and he's a Treasury Agent) but each think the other is part of a criminal drug smuggling ring. That poses complications for Johnny McEvoy (played by Fred MacMurray) and Madeleine Haley (Claire Trevor) who fall in love as, posing as husband and wife, they race to stay ahead of drug dealer Pete Ritchie (Raymond Burr). Here's the layout: both the Feds and the local police want to find out who's the kingpin behind Ritchie's distribution network. Working separately, the police send Haley to work her womanly charms on Ritchie while the Feds manage to place McEvoy in a rival gang. Haley is caught searching Ritchie's apartment but then Ritchie is caught flatfooted by McEvoy. Escaping, McEvoy takes Haley with him to the gang leader he's working for and she's forced to cooperate posing as McEvoy's wife as they smuggle a shipment of heroine into the US. Along the way, they fall in love both knowing all the while that they'll have turn in the other to authorities at the border. Director William Selter keeps the action full speed ahead while the script by Devery Freeman is sharp, concise, and clever in its repartee. ("We need a cheap, tawdry dame," says a police detective planning to use a woman to ingratiate herself onto Ritchie. "She can handle it," replies another cop, indicating Haley) The film's two leading men are noir favorites headlined by MacMurray whose clipped, no nonsense style contrasts well against Trevor's naive demeanor. (Her portrayal of a night club dancer early in the film is hilarious in its lack of subtlety) And the film's heavy (no pun intended!) Raymond Burr hardly has to strain himself in the role of the humorless Ritchie. So does Selter succeed in balancing the romcom against the hard boiled elements? He does, making *Borderline* a little seen but must see film in the noir cannon!

Madeleine Haley (Claire Trevor) makes a play for drug kingpin Pete Ritchie (Raymond Burr

116

In a race to the border, Madeleine Haley (Claire Trevor) and Johnny McEvoy (Fred MacMurray) struggle not to fall in love

In a scene reminiscent of *It Happened One Night*, Madellaine and Johnny play house as "husband and wife"

Side Street (1950)

Director Anthony Mann strikes again with a film noir of the classic kind! This time, he has down on his luck mailman Joe Norson (played by Farley Granger) tempted to steal $30,000 from the office of crooked lawyer Victor Backet (Edmund Ryan). Living with his wife's parents, Joe needs the dough to make life easier for spouse Ellen (Cathy O'Donnell) and cover the cost of a private room at the hospital so that she can have their baby in comfort. But after a while, his conscience begins to bother him and he attempts to return the money but instead only triggers a series of events that leaves a trail of dead bodies in their wake. Caught in the middle of it, Joe gets in deeper and deeper after he discovers that the bartender with whom he's entrusted the money has absconded with it. In trying to get it back, he manages to stay one jump ahead of the killers but is eventually caught. He ends up in a wild car chase and hospitalized for his trouble but is left by scriptwriter Sydney Boehm with some light at the end of the tunnel preventing him from suffering the ultimate fate of the classic noir protagonist. Enough can't be said of the film's twisty, ever deepening plot nor Mann's sure direction that's aided immeasurably by location shooting entirely on the streets of 1940s Manhattan and Brooklyn with its crowded streets, trashy alleys, dingy store fronts, and broad, skyscraper lined avenues. In fact, the film begins with hypnotic aerial shots of the city before ending at ground level with one of the first and most elaborate car chases ever filmed up to that time. In between, Mann's individual layups (with the help of cinematographer Joseph Ruttenberg) are exactly framed and balanced, often with views down long streets with towering buildings centered at the end. Granger and O'Donnell make the perfect couple with Granger showing just the right amount of fear, confusion, and torment as an ordinary guy who makes that one fateful mistake. We know that because the narration by police Capt. Walter Anderson (Paul Kelly) tells us so. It's Anderson's calm reassurance that compels viewers to believe that right and order will out and that the law will make sure that good folks like the Norson's who get caught up in crime's web will find justice. A must see!

Desperation and fear can be plainly seen on Farley Granger's face as he's taken for a ride by killers looking for the missing money

The conclusion of one of the first great car chase scenes in cinema as Joe Norson comes to the end of his noir sojourn...directly in front of the New York Stack Exchange!

Jean Hagen provides some eye candy while Kathy O'Donnell is stuck in the hospital; but not for long! Her murder will place even more pressure on the hapless Joe

Tension (1950)

A film that begins as a domestic tragedy with milquetoast husband Warren Quimby (played by Richard Basehart) being played for a patsy by his hot to trot wife who plays around with other men without even bothering to hide it from her husband. But Warren is so pathetically hooked on Claire (and no wonder, she's played by noir queen Audrey Totter) that he meekly accepts not only her wanton ways but her outright disgust for him. When she finds a man who can fulfill her dreams of easy living (brutish Barney Deager played by Lloyd Gough), she packs her bags and gives Warren the brush off. Working up the gumption to confront Deager, Warren is beaten up for his trouble. He seethes in impotent anger until he comes up with the idea of establishing a new identity and using it to kill Deager thus leaving no trail for the police to follow. Under the anonymity supplied by his new identity as Paul Sothern, Warren finds himself a new man as well. Suddenly, he becomes bolder, braver and not only masters Deager but wins the love of next door neighbor Mary Chanler (Cyd Charisse). That's when the roof falls in. It happens when he makes that one noirish wrong decision: when Deager is murdered by parties unknown, Claire returns and threatens to turn him in to the cops. At that point, Warren buckles and goes along with the coverup. Enter Barry Sullivan as Det. Collier Bonnabel who immediately suspects the pair. And though no one can blame him from playing up to sexy Claire, Bonnabel tricks her into revealing that she was the one who killed Deagar after all. (The reason isn't clear; did he confront her after she began to cheat on him too?) Director John Berry keeps the film moving along but is helped most especially by Allen Rivkin whose script barely has a dull moment in it. A strong cast helps too led off by Basehart who couldn't turn in a bad performance in these years. He's convincing both as the weak husband and the confident Sothern and then the weak husband again! Totter is perfect as the two timing wife and Charisse surprises in a straight acting role, her appearance considerably toned down from her more glamorous roles in musicals. Sullivan works well as the emotionless Bonnabel who also narrates this sordid tale of infidelity and murder. Some modest location shooting around Los Angeles helps with the noirish atmosphere. With all that going for it, it comes as a shock to realize that this forgotten gem didn't turn a profit for its studio!

Warren Quimby (Richard Basehart) looks on helplessly as Barney Deager (Lloyd Gough) dallies with Quimby's wife Claire (Audrey Totter)

Mary Chanler (Cyd Charisse) and Warren Quimby are questioned by a suspicious Det. Collier Bonnabel (Gene Barry)

Audrey Totter on the set of *Tension*

Where Danger Lives (1950)

Dr. Jeff Cameron (played by Robert Mitchum) has it all: a winning bedside manner, the respect of his peers, and engagement to an attractive nurse (Maureen O'Sullivan). He soon throws it all away in the best noir tradition when he finds himself assigned to a new patient, the beautiful and wildly desirable Margo Lannington (Faith Domergue). Almost immediately, his fortunes take a downward spiral after he forms an unhealthy attraction to the mentally unbalanced Margo. It begins when he makes the unwise decision to make a house call on Margo (just to see how she's getting along you understand). Well, one thing leads to another and the two fall in love. Then, one day, Jeff decides to clear the air with Margo's father only to discover that he's not her father but her husband! Angry with Margo, he leaves the house but there's a scream. He goes back and finds that Frederick (Claude Rains) has apparently torn an earring from Margo's bleeding ear. There's a struggle with a poker. Jeff is struck in the head and Frederick falls also hitting his head. Jeff stumbles from the room to wash up and when he returns, finds that Frederick is dead. He suggests calling the police, but Margo convinces him that they'll never believe it wasn't murder so with no other option they go on the lam. What follows is a series of incidents that find the pair getting worse and worse off with Jeff suffering from concussion. At one point, they're forced by circumstances to go through with marriage (demanded by the production code) and finally hit rock bottom in a dingy apartment on the Mexican border. There, a delirious Jeff is shot by Margo and left for dead as she tries to make it across the border on her own. Director John Farrow keeps things moving along, preventing viewers from catching their breaths and the script by Charles Bennett is flawless noir. In fact, there are few film noir that get as black as *Where Danger Lives*. The only thing missing was for Jeff to die. Unfortunately perhaps, studio heads may have nixed such an unhappy ending. As it is, Margo is the one who ends up toast. Mitchum, usually cast as stoic tough guys, is excellent as the easy going doctor and the lovesick boob and Faith Domergue is...well Faith Domergue! Sexy and svelt, it was easy to see what Howard Hughes saw in her! Cinematography by Nicholas Musuraca does noir proud here from the nighted city streets to small town shindig to seemy border town sliminess. In between is the stark desert environment through which the psychotic Margo and the delirious Jeff must travel before reaching the imagined safety of Mexico. Terrific film!

He used to be a human being once dept: Jeff Cameron (Robert Mitchum) already looks to be at the end of his rope in this scene with the conniving Margo Lannington (Faith Domergue)

Unusual camera angle as Margo Lannington (Faith Domergue) is held by Jeff Cameron (Robert Mitchum) upon the apparently accidental death of Frederick Lannington (foreground)

Irresistable: Faith Domergue

Where the Sidewalk Ends (1950)

Story of a New York City police detective with a reputation for brutality. In fact, the film opens with Det. Mark Dixon (played by Dana Andrews) called on the carpet for just that. He's demoted and sent back out on the streets where he becomes involved with the investigation of the murder of a man who won too much at a private crap game held by gang boss Tommy Scalisi (Gary Merrill). Sent to look up the murder suspect (Craig Stevens), Dixon ends up accidentally killing him when the man attacks him and he's forced to hit back. Fearful about losing his job and going to jail, Dixon arrives at his noir decision point and makes the wrong one: he decides to cover up the killing. Shortly after that, he meets the dead man's attractive widow, Morgan Paine (Gene Tierney) even as her father is falsely accused of Dixon's crime. With his affection for Morgan growing, Dixon's conscience really begins to bother him. He tries to hire a high powered lawyer to defend Morgan's father but the plan falls through. In desperation, he tries to make Scalisi look like the guilty party and deliberately sets himself up to be shot by the gangster. But one of Scalisi's hoods talks under police questioning and ties Scalisi with the Paine murder. Dixon is in the clear. But that conscience still won't let him alone. He ends up revealing the truth to his boss who promptly has him arrested. Will Morgan wait for him to finish his prison sentence? That's left up in the air in a near perfect finish for a film noir. Shot partially on location in New York by cinematographer Joseph LaShelle (with some really spectacular night shots of elevated trains and the silhouetted George Washington Bridge), *Where the Sidewalk Ends* is a fast moving, intriguing thriller directed by Otto Preminger that combines early proto-noir detective fiction with true noir descent and redemption themes. The re-teaming of Andrews and Tierney following their earlier film, *Laura*, is good with Andrews excellent as the brutal cop, but Tierney is just too glamorous to be believable as the struggling daughter of a cab driver.

Det. Mark Dixon (Dana Andrews) confronts gang leader Tommy Scalisi (Gary Merrill) trying to set him up as the murderer

Det. Mark Dixon (Dana Andrews) arrives at his noir decision point: to cover up or not to cover up?

When pressed glamorous Gene Tierney could manage to look like a taxi driver's daughter

The Asphalt Jungle (1950)

The second greatest heist film of all time (after *The Killing* which, coincidentallly or not, also starred Sterling Hayden), and in the tradition of film noir, nobody comes out smelling like a rose. Least of all Dix Handley (played by the taciturn Hayden) a Kentucky lunk who dreams of hitting it big enough to bankroll his return to the farm his family once owned. To do it, he makes one mistake after another (every time he gets a couple nickels to rub together he bets on the ponies...and loses) until, down on his luck, he falls in with a gang planning a jewel theft worth a million dollars. It proves to be his last mistake as the heist goes wrong and he ends up shot after a confrontation with the gang's untrustworthy front man. Hayden is perfectly cast as the hardened but sympathetic Handley and Sam Jaffe couldn't be better as Erwin "Doc" Riedenschneider, the brains of the outfit whose obsession with young girls spells his downfall. James Whitmore as the hunchbacked Gus Minissi, who overcompensates to prove how tough he is, ticking like a time bomb that could explode at any minute and does in a wild jail cell scene. Jean Hagen is suitably pathetic as Dix hanger on Doll Conovan and Louis Calhern is smooth as high end backer and double crosser, Alonzo D. Emmerich. Finally, the topper on the excellent casting is Marilyn Monroe in one of her earliest roles and perhaps her most adorable look. She doesn't have a big part, but those she has as Emmerich's plaything Angela Phinlay, are arresting. As usual in noir films, the story by Ben Maddow and John Huston (who also directed) is told in such a way that the viewer often sides with the criminal or the hapless schlep who makes that fatal mistake. Such is the case with Dix whose dream is to return to the farm where he grew up and that singleminded desire is the only thing that keeps him going after being shot by Emmerich's henchman, Bob Brannom (Brad Dexter; don't blink or you'll miss him!). Huston's direction is as flawless as the casting with the heist scenes depicted in a mostly wordless sequence that underlines the gang's professionalism. But the action never overwhelms the characterization. Every member of the gang as well as Emmerich, Shinlay, and Brannom have their moments to shine along with bit parts for a number of other minor characters. Cinematography by Harold Rosson is sharp, equally capturing the dingy hideouts and apartments of the low rent gangsters and their supporters as well as the richer surroundings of Emmerich's home and summer cottage. It all adds up to excitement, danger, and suspense and is well deserving of its reputation as one of the best film noirs ever.

Erwin "Doc" Riedenschneider (Sam Jaffe back to camera) lays out the plan to Dix Handley (Sterling Hayden) and the unstable Gus Minissi (James Whitmore standing)

Marilyn Monroe, at her most delicious, made one of her earliest appearances in *The Asphalt Jungle*

It all goes south: Thieves fall out among themselves following an imperfect heist

Sunset Boulevard (1950)

Intriguing and in some ways horrific noir co-scripted and directed by Billy Wilder that begins with the discovery of a body in the pool of an ornate, neglected mansion located on Hollywood's Sunset Boulevard. The catch is that the dead man is narrating the story and the presentation of his body at the very start of the film sets the viewer to wondering how it got there not necessarily how he was killed (shot three times as the narrator reveals right at the start) The dead man is struggling screenwriter and reluctant gigolo Joe Gillis (played by William Holden) who finds himself a guest in the home of faded and nearly forgotten silent screen star Norma Desmond (Gloria Swanson). In short order, Joe is hired by Norma to help in writing her comeback film script but never sees any of the money he's promised. Instead, he's steered from his room over the garage into a bedroom adjoining Norma's, rooms whose doors have no locks. As the weeks pass, Joe becomes a kept man with all his wants and needs paid for. And when Norma attempts suicide after he threatens to leave, he comes back not only to the house but into her bed. Meanwhile, in an excursion to the outside world, he meets pretty Betty Schaefer (Nancy Olson) an aspiring screenwriter and they begin a clandestine partnership one that quickly leads to love. Discovering his infidelity, Norma calls Betty and tells her the truth about Joe. Caught, Joe decides to come clean and invites Betty to the mansion where he reveals all. Finally, in a fit of self-loathing, he splits with Betty and packs up to leave Norma telling her that everything she believes about herself is delusion. Driven to desperation at the thought of losing Gillis, Norma shoots him and he tumbles into the pool. But the film doesn't end there. There's an epilogue as the now fully mad Norma, surrounded by police and TV cameras, imagines she's back at work on a movie as she descends the stairs, her painted face the last thing viewers see as it blurs in a final, useless close up. Joe's plunge from struggling scriptwriter to trapped and humiliated house puppy to boy toy, to his doomed effort to free himself from Norma's clutches, to his death follows the classic noir glide path with Holden's cynical portrayal of the hapless, weak willed Joe a convincing performance. Early film star Gloria Swanson is cloying, demanding, and pathetic all at the same time but it's Erich von Stroheim's under played role as Max van Mayerling, Norma's chauffeur, butler, keeper, and ex-husband that stands out. Stroheim, one of the silent era's greatest and most outrageous directors, was joined by other early Hollywood characters such as H.G. Warner (who played Jesus in the silent version of *The Greatest Story Ever Told*), Buster Keaton, and Cecil B. DeMille in adding a sense of versimilitude to the goings on. Also adding to the realism, were location shoots in downtown Los Angeles, use of the Paramount Studios lot, and the famous Schwab's Drugstore. Cinematography by John Seitz called for mostly night scenes but his lighting for Norma's gloomy, run down, mansion made it a character in and of itself. The scene where Norma and Max conduct burial rites for Norm'a pet chimp is downright strange. Filled with weird scenes, grotesque imagery, and a deadening sense of gloom and despair, *Sunset Boulevard* is a must see for all fans of film noir!

Creepy Norma Desmond (Gloria Swanson) makes her final pitch for the cameras

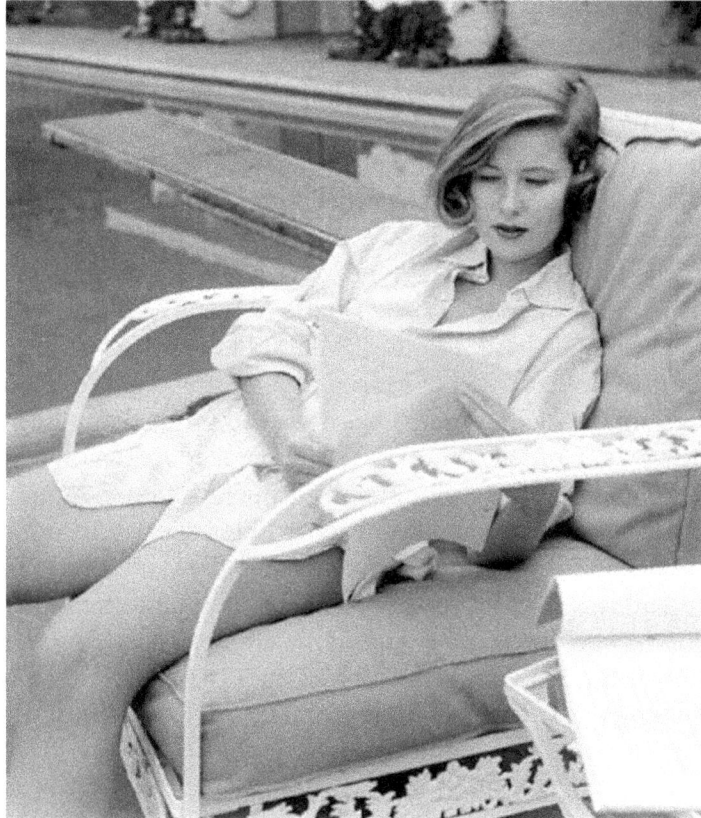

Nancy Olsen studies her lines for *Sunset Boulevard*...a definite improvement over Gloria Swanson's Norma Desmond!

The body of Joe Gillis is found in Norma Desmond's pool at the start of *Sunset Boulevard*

Armored Car Robbery (1950)

A heist film in which a gang of thieves plans the perfect crime: robbing an armored car as it is waiting for the day's take outside a capacity crowd sports stadium. Headed by perfectionist and ultra wary Dave Purvis (a pre-*Perry Mason* William Talman), the gang also includes noir regular Steve Brodie as gang member Al Mapes. But even the most well laid plans of mice and men can go awry when a dame's thrown into the mix and that's what happens here when, unbeknownst to gang member Benny McBride (Douglas Fowley), Purvis is seeing his strip teaser wife, Yvonne, on the side. Together, the two intend to run away together after the job. As luck would have it, McBride catches a bullet when the heist goes south and interfering cops (headed by noir favorite Charles McGraw as Lt. Jim Cordell) break it up. At their hideout, the desperate criminals have a falling out amid mutual suspicion, especially after Purvis puts Benny out of his misery. They split up but Mapes is determined not to let Purvis get away with all the loot. He tracks down Yvonne (Adele Jergens) but is picked up by the police before he can get any information out of her. However, Cordell, following police procedure, catch up to Purvis and his amour at the airport and the film concludes with a familiar noir trope: the stolen money blowing in the wind propelled by a plane's jet wash. Filmed by director Richard Fleischer on location in Los Angeles (the stadium where the hold up occurs was Wrigley Field) and shot by Guy Roe in high contrast style, the story is fast moving at a breathless 67 minutes and thus, has no time for let up. Talman turns out to be perfect as the paranoid Purvis who cuts the tags out of his clothes and changes addresses constantly to keep from being known or identified by police. And McGraw is equally well cast as the dogged, bulldog of a cop, a role he'd reprise often in his career. Fun.

There's always a dame around to mess things up: Dave Purvis (William Tallman) and Yvonne McBride (Adele Jurgens) plan betrayal and murder

On the other hand, if you gotta risk everything for a dame, you could do worse than Adele Jurgens!

Heist in progress: The gang knocks off an armored car. After that, things go south

Southside 1-1000 (1950)

Noir but strictly in the police procedural mode opening with a virtual mini-documentary on the nature and usefulness of money and proceeding from there with a narrator driven story line involving Treasury agents going undercover to track down a counterfeiting ring. That said, the no nonsense directing by Boris Ingster (who?!) is good and locations in and around Los Angeles (especially the rather odd looking Angels Flight cable car service) really helped. In particular, the climactic fight scene as lead agent John Riggs (Don DeFore) confronts femme fatale and ringleader Nora Craig (Andrea King) on the cable car overpass was impressive. Also noteworthy was Defore himself, who comports himself well in the serious role of the Treasury agent attempting the dangerous task of infiltrating the counterfeit ring. Known mostly for light or comedic roles, DeFore convinces as the tough agent who becomes romantically involved with Craig only to find out she's the head of the ring. Craig finds herself in charge by virtue of being the daughter of Eugene Deane (Morris Ankrum), a prison inmate who secretly creates the plates from which the counterfeit money will be printed. It's after they're smuggled out of prison and used to print money that Riggs becomes involved in the case as the documentary style story unfolds showing the step by step process the Department uses to track down the counterfeiters. (It was based on a true story after all) The balance of the cast is a name dropper's dream. Populated with such Hollywood character actors such as George Tobias who gets to push Bill Kelly out a twentieth story window! One small misstep, an unlikely turn of events that exposes Riggs to the gang, is when Craig receives a notebook of doodles drawn by her father one of which is of Riggs identified as a Treasury agent. Who knew Morris Ankrum was an amateur caricaturist? But the only real downside to the movie is the end credits which feature possibly the most inappropriate exit music ever to grace a film noir coming as it does immediately following Craig's messy death beneath the wheels of a cable car. Eww!

Careful Don! She's murder!

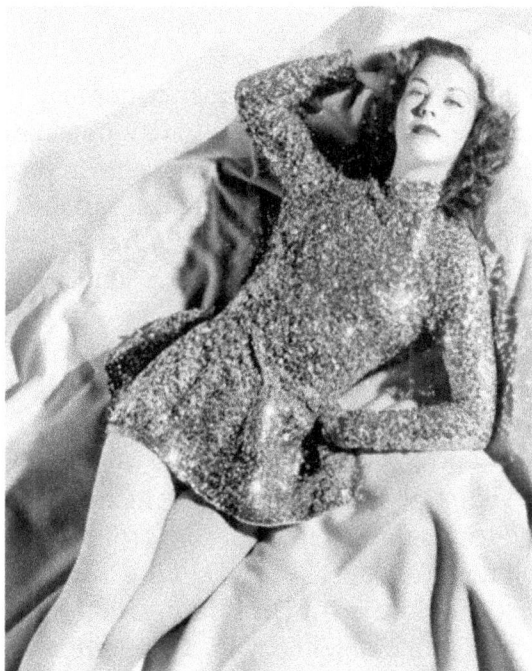

Easy to fall for: Perfectly understandable why John Riggs could be led astray by Andrea King

**Nice noirish shot by director Boris Ingster of Nora Craig (Andrea King)
behind a rain spattered window**

Quicksand (1950)

For a perfect example of film noir, a viewer can't find much better than the aptly named *Quicksand*, directed by Irving Pichel and starring Micky Rooney in a career transitioning role as Dan, the hapless garage mechanic. In fact, in order to transition from his clean cut youthful image of Andy Hardy days, Rooney co-financed this picture as a starring vehicle for himself. In the title role, he falls hard for bad girl Vera (played by Jeanne Cagney). As a result, he cribs $20 from the till at the garage where he works which then becomes his noir decision point. From there, one thing leads to another until Dan hits rock bottom. Although he intended to replace the money, events outpace Dan and before he knows it he's sinking into the mire first with revenue agents chasing him down for pawning a watch under false pretenses, then rolling a drunk of his money, then being blackmailed by Nick (Peter Lorre) who threatens to turn him over to the police unless he gives him a new car. Desperate, Dan steals a car from the garage where he works but then is threatened again by the owner if he doesn't cough up twice the amount it's worth. Confiding in Vera, Dan learns where Nick hides his profits from the pinball parlor he operates. Stealing the money and leaving it in Vera's care, he returns only to find that Vera has gone out and spent half of it to buy herself a mink coat! The rat! Dan finally hits bottom when he confronts the garage owner and strangles him. (The close up of Dan's face with the dazed, bewildered look, like a trapped animal, is classic) Now he's on the run, in a wild attempt to reach Mexico and safety. Whew! Throughout, he's dogged by good girl Helen (Barbara Bates) even though he threw her to the curb after being dazzled by bad girl Vera. By the end, he realizes his mistake but it's too late, even though it turns out he didn't kill the garage owner, he's going to spend the next ten years in the pen. The good news is that the long suffering Helen will wait for him. (The only thing that keeps this film from being a total out and out noir classic is the fact that Dan survives...a perfect noir would have had him killed in the end. Oh, well) Shot at a hectic pace on locations around Los Angeles, the film totally succeeds in Rooney's aim: to transform him from an ingenue to a fully rounded adult actor. One of the very best film noir ever!

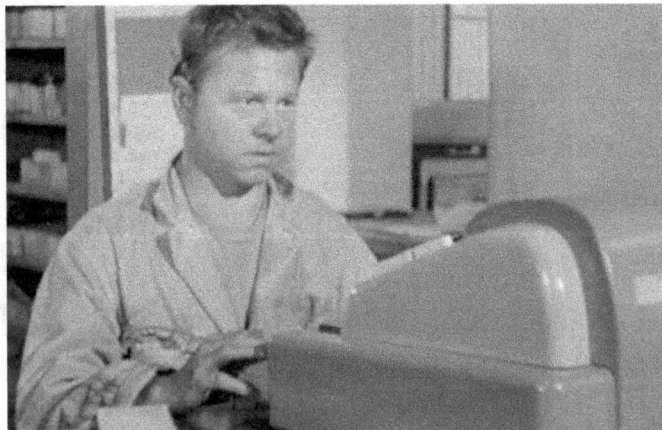

The first domino falls: Dan (Mickey Rooney) makes his big mistake, taking $20 from the till just so he could show bad girl Vera a good time

Jeanne Cagney didn't usually portray bad girls but she could if needed.

On the run from the law, Dan, with Helen in tow, carjacks an innocent bystander who ends up giving them some good advice

Gun Crazy (1950)

Although produced as a low budget, independent feature, *Gun Crazy* has turned out to be one of the best all out film noirs of all time! It tells the sordid tale of Bart Tare (played by John Dall) and Annie Laurie Starr (Peggy Cummins) as they tear across the southwest on a crime spree fueled by their mutual love of guns and each other. The film begins with an opening sequence with the youthful Bart (played by "Rusty" Tamblyn in one of his earliest roles) breaking into a gun shop to steal a revolver. But viewers are misdirected when they're led to believe that the movie is going to be about Bart's unhealthy attraction to guns, a theme explored in MacKinlay Kantor's original story but more or less abandoned by screenwriter Dalton Trumbo. Instead, when the film shifts to the grown up Bart, guns become mere phallic devices as the emphasis in tone shifts from the psychological to psycho-sexual. This aspect of the film wasn't lost on director Joseph Lewis who admitted in an interview that his instructions to Dall and Cummins was that they were virtually dogs in heat. In the days when the production code still had teeth, director and actors could only go so far but what they did manage to put on screen left no doubt that far more was on the characters' minds than simple gunplay. But there was subtlety too as Bart is plagued by a conscience that not only rebelled against the idea of a life of crime but also of murder something that Annie actually delights in. But sex overwhelms any pangs of guilt Bart might have as he allows himself to go along with every whim made by the demanding Annie. In one scene that captures Bart's dilemma, after he talks about quitting their lives of crime Annie, wrapped in a bathrobe, stretches herself out on the bed and says if he quits, she'll leave him. Like a filing to a magnet, Bart is drawn to her reclining figure and wordlessly surrenders in her arms. But the ultimate expression of his sexual attachment to Annie comes at the conclusion of the pair's robbery of a plant payroll. Planning to split up for a few months until the heat is off, they get into two separate cars and begin driving in different directions. Suddenly they both stop, look back, and then make U turns back. The cars barely have enough time to come to a full stop before Bart throws his things into Annie's car, and jumping in beside her, immediately falls into a mad, orgiastic clinch. And talk about perfect casting! Cummins smoulders as Annie convincing viewers that indeed, she could make any male do whatever she wanted him to do. And Dall, whose grinning, aw shucks attitude perfectly captures Bart's naivete that makes him putty in Annie's hands. From the time they meet in a sideshow shooting contest it's a downward spiral into the darkest pits of film noir with Annie, a murder and seduction already under her belt, and the sex stupid Bart on different paths that ultimately come together in a hungry passion that neither of them can control. The film itself moves like a bullet from one scene to another punctuated by the couple's cowboy themed holdups of which the high point comes in an unbroken three and half minute sequence taken from inside the getaway car. *Gun Crazy* or *Sex Crazy* this one's for the books!

**Annie and Bart make their getaway as director Joseph Lewis films
the holdup sequence in a long, single take**

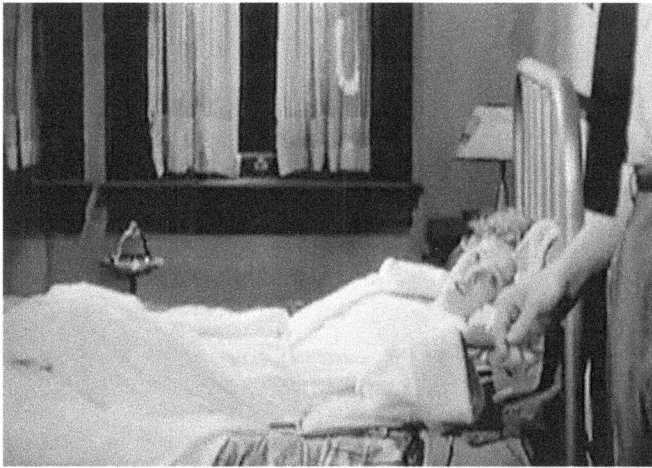

Bart has a crisis of conscience that's soon forgotten as Annie lies back and reminds him about what he'd lose if he quits...

The smoldering Peggy Cummins made all too few films for Hollywood

The girl and the gun that drove Bart crazy

Night and the City (1950)

London locations are somewhat disorienting for a noir setting as con man Harry Fabian (played by Richard Widmark) is convinced that he's finally hit on the real thing: making a fortune on big time wrestling! The only problem is that the circuit is controlled by gangster Kristo (Herbert Lom) who doesn't appreciate Fabian muscling in on the racket. But there's nothing much he can do about it since Fabian's ace in the hole is Gregorius the Great (Stanislau Zbyszko) who also happens to be Kristo's father! Further complications involve Fabian's lack of funds which he acquires from Helen Noseross (Googie Withers) the wife of Silver Fox Club owner Phil Noseross (Francis L. Sullivan) a shady character who loves a wife who doesn't love him back. Scheming with Kristo, Phil also gives Fabian money only to yank it at the last minute figuring it would put him out of business. But Fabian turns the tables on him, persuading Gregorius to fight the Strangler (Mike Mazurki) in a contest of traditional Greco style wrestling versus the crass modern kind. But when the two meet at the gym, tempers flare and a no holds barred fight erupts. After one of the most brutal fight scenes ever filmed, Gregorius emerges the victor but dies from the exertion soon after. Now Fabian's goose is well and goodly cooked! With Kristo's hands now free, he unleashes the entire London underworld on Fabian who's finally cornered with girlfriend Mary Bristol (Gene Tierney). But their relationship is doomed as Fabian breaks cover yelling that Mary betrayed him hoping that she can at least profit from his death by collecting the bounty placed on him by Kristo. In true noir style, no one ends up well in this film with Fabian caught and killed by the Strangler; the Strangler arrested on a murder charge; Kristo's father, Gregorius dead; Phil commits suicide; and Helen, after discovering that the license Fabian gave her is a forgery, drags herself back to Phil only to learn that he killed himself and left everything not to her but to the club's old cleaning woman. It was as convoluted a plot as one could figure scripted by one Jo Esinger, directed beautifully by Jules Dassin, and lit by Max Greene. And there was no day for night stuff either as Greene takes full advantage of the London locations to capture the back alleys, rotting wharves, and fog slick streets of the city in all their run down glory. And though New York or Chicago or Los Angeles could have done just as easily, the London settings didn't hurt *Night and the City* at all. Widmark is perfect casting for a small time con man in over his head and Mazurki was born to play the Strangler. Gene Tierney however, was virtually superfluous as nightclub songbird and Widmark's love interest. Nothing much was done with her other than being there for Widmark to steal from. Likewise Hugh Marlowe as upstairs neighbor Adam Dunne who's sweet on Tierney but whose arc goes nowhere. On the other hand, Zbyszko as the unsuspecting Gregorius and Withers as the luckless Helen are the real standouts. Recommended.

Harry Fabian (Richard Widmark) keeping one step ahead of the underworld at the climax to *Night and the City*

Harry Fabian isn't the only one that ends up badly in *Night and the City*; so does the scheming Helen Noseross (Googie Withers) and love sick husband Phil Noseross (Francis L. Sullivan)-

Far from distracting the noir purist, the London settings don't hurt *Night and the City* at all

Mystery Street (1950)

This police procedural keeps viewers guessing about how Lt. Peter Morales gets from point A to point B as he tries to solve the murder of a local prostitute. Directed by John Sturges and filmed on location in Boston, Massachusetts, including scenes of Harvard University, Hyannis, and various neighborhoods in the city, atmosphere is created with establishing shots and often darkened, night time photography by John Alton. One shot of ornithologist Walter Burke running along the beach after discovering a body is beautiful. The noir element comes in when young husband Henry Shanway (Marshall Thompson) gets drunk one night after his wife loses their baby in a miscarriage. He's picked up by b girl Vivian Helding (Jan Sterling) who needs his car for transportation. She drives them out to a remote area, dumps the hapless Henry, and meets the John who's left her pregnant. She's killed for her trouble and the unknown killer buries her body on the beach. Shanway's car is sunk in a bog. Weeks later, Vivian's bones are discovered and delivered to Harvard's medical school for examination by one Dr. McAdoo (Bruce Bennett). That's when Morales (played by Ricardo Montalban against type) is given the assignment. From there, the two go from clue to clue, building a case against Henry who reaches his noir decision point only to take a wrong turn. He lies about his involvement with Vivian. But when it's discovered that Vivian was shot, Morales begins to doubt that Henry is the killer. Meanwhile, Vivian's shady landlady (Elsa Lanchester) has beat the cops to the real killer, found the murder weapon, and attempts blackmail. The story by Sydney Boehm and Richard Brooks is compelling and builds quickly with all the pieces fitting together. Montalban is a different type of police detective being on his first murder case and learning as he goes while also being a member of a minority group that one didn't see too much on film in these years. Thompson is good as the accused caught in a web only partially of his own making. The film also has a number of strong parts for women as well with Sally Forrest as Grace Shanway, still grieving for her lost child while angry at police who've accused her husband of murder; Betsy Blair, Vivian's conscientious neighbor who slings hash when she's not being handy with automatics; Elsa Lanchester as the scheming landlady; and Sterling as the bleached blond b girl with a little book full of names. Highly recommended!

Lt. Peter Morales (Recardo Montalban) discusses details of his first murder investigation with fellow officers.

Who'd believe husband Henry could cheat on a wife who   looked like Sally Forrest?

Part procedural, part detective fiction, *Mystery Street* spends as much time in the
lab as it does on the gumshoe trail

The Man Who Cheated Himself (1950)

Representative of another film noir trope, namely the dirty cop who ends up hoisted on his own petard, *The Man Who Cheated Himself* is Lt. Edward Cullen (Lee J. Cobb) who makes the mistake of falling for high class divorcee Lois Frazer (Jane Wyatt) With her husband supposedly out of town, Cullen hooks up with Lois. It's then that things begin to happen as the husband surprises them and Lois shoots him. What to do? Either Cullen turns in his lover and ruins his own career or just doesn't report the crime. Of course, he makes the wrong choice and dumps the body at the local airport and the murder weapon into the bay. Complicating matters is that his brother Andy has partnered with him at the office and they end up having to investigate the case of Lois' husband together. As his brother (played by John Dall) unknowingly closes in on the killer (namely his own brother) a false lead appears to solve the case. But Dall has nagging suspicions and ends up making the reluctant conclusion that his brother is the killer. Fast forward to the end, after Cullen has been arrested. He's waiting outside the courtroom to be arraigned and Lois walks by with her high powered attorney and ignoring Cullen as if he doesn't exist. The suggestion is she's going to get off while Cullen heads up the river. Hoo boy! Solid direction by Felix Feist takes advantage of San Francisco locations climaxing with scenes shot at Fort Point located directly beneath the Golden Gate Bridge. A fast moving script by Seton Miller and Philip MacDonald and a good cast doesn't let him down. Worth catching!

Location shooting at Fort Point for *The Man Who Cheated Himself* gave the film a million dollars in added production value!

In deep: With police at the door, Lt. Edward Cullen (Lee J. Cobb) must decide either to report the murder and ruin his career or cover it up

Edward Cullen (Lee J. Cobb) and brother Andy (John Dall) find a gun that seemingly leads the investigation

The Mob (1951)

Broderick Crawford is police detective Johnny Damico who has the misfortune of witnessing a murder and letting the killer get away under the impression that the man was a fellow officer. A relatively straightforward tale as Damico goes undercover to find the murderer undergoing the usual trials by members of the mob and earning their trust thereby. The film's main claim to fame is its cast. Besides Crawford, there's mob enforcer Neville Brand, mob leader Ernest Borgnine, noir regular Richard Kiley, and an uncredited early appearance by Charles Bronson as a dockhand. Direction by Robert Parrish is good with some nice location work especially on the docks with gritty cinematography by Joseph Walker.

Going undercover, Johnny Damico (Broderick Crawford) poses as a dock wollaper and meets noir regular Richard Kiley (right) and Charles Bronson (far right) in an early role

In with the mob, Johnny still isn't able to shake the suspicions of mob enforcer Gunner (Neville Brand)

Johnny is vetted by the mob including boss Joe Castro (Ernest Borgnine)

Unlike most noir femmes, Betty Beuhler wasn't much to look at, but her nurse Mary Kiernan gave bulldog Johnny something to look forward to when the danger ended

Ace in the Hole (1951)

Kirk Douglas plays down on his luck news reporter Chuck Tatum who stumbles onto the story of a lifetime. Eager to strike it so big, the eastern papers that fired him would be begging for him to come back, Tatum recognizes that a man caught in a cave-in could be milked for days, maybe weeks until the whole nation becomes mesmerized by his plight. Proceeding on that assumption, Tatum brings in corrupt local politicians and convinces them to dig where it will take the longest to reach the trapped Leo Minosa. As crowds gather and grow bigger and bigger, Minosa's faithless wife packs her bags to leave him until she realizes how much money there is to be made at her husband's expense. She stays to operate her cafe/souvenir stand and plays up to Tatum. In the meantime, Tatum's cold blooded plan works. The eastern papers take notice and begin calling and offering him more and more. But then, Tatum's plan is blown sky high when Minosa dies before he can be rescued. Through his own selfishness, Tatum finds himself not only back where he started, but wracked by guilt over Minosa's death. In a confrontation with Minosa's wife, there's a struggle and he's stabbed. Dying, he makes his way back to the local newspaper office that hired him and falls dead on the floor, his face landing such that it fills the camera in the movie's final, shocking scene. Written, produced, and directed by Billy Wilder, *Ace in the Hole* is a condemnation of the American press with its appetite for sensation and habit of going on to the next story carelessly leaving shattered lives in its wake. That point is brilliantly expressed by the circus-like atmosphere surrounding the cave-in victim with its sideshow tents, country music performances, souvenir selling, and huge crowds of curious onlookers that by the picture's end, are streaming out of trains heading for the spectacle. Douglas is perfect in the role of Tatum; his frenetic self aggrandizement and faux sincerity when dealing with the trapped Minosa is totally believable. Jan Sterling, meanwhile, as Lorraine Minosa, is convincingly shallow and insincere. While the film doesn't fulfill the strict definition of noir, it certainly fills the bill in its nihilism and the shady nature of Tatum and his just desserts. See it.

Chuck Tatum (Kirk Douglas) presides as MC over the circus-like atmosphere that has built up around the victim of a cave in

Tatem works to keep cave in victim Leo Minosa's spirits up while awaiting rescue; one that would arrive too late

Jan Sterling was perfect casting for Minosa's faithless wife

Fourteen Hours (1951)

Not a traditonal noir, *Fourteen Hours* tells the story of Robert Cosick (Richard Basehart) a disturbed young man determined to commit suicide by leaping from the fifteenth floor of a New York Hotel. Basehart is perfect as the diffident young man and Paul Douglas (as police officer Charlie Dunnigan) as the grizzled beat cop who first comes across him and then plays a key role in trying to keep Cosick calm and convincing him not to jump. Directed by Henry Hathaway, the film presents a convincing look at the hectic behind the scenes activity of the police in dealing with such cases even as the script avoided the expected flashbacks to tell the story in straight time and how the drama effects other people in Cosick's orbit including Grace Kelly in her debut as a woman in the throes of divorce; Jeffrery Hunter and Debra Paget as a young couple who meet and fall in love during the fourteen hour ordeal; Barbara Bel Geddes as Cosick's estranged girlfriend; Agnes Moorehead as Cosick's self absorbed mother; Robert Keith as Cosick's guilt ridden father (whose real life son Brian Keith also had a bit part in crowd scenes); Howard da Silva as the harried police chief in charge of the operation; and Jeff Corey as the policeman who almost grabbed Cosick as he came back inside only to be frightened back out by the sudden appearance of a religious kook. Also on hand in bit parts were Ossie Davis, Brad Dexter, Richard Beymer, and John Cassavetes. But another character in the film goes uncredited: that of New York City itself. The movie really gives the viewer a sense of place in its breathtaking shots both at street level and skyline that are seamlessly integrated into the action. Based on a true story, the script by John Paxton keeps the viewer riveted for the entire 92 minute run time. Recommended.

Virginia Foster (Barbara Bel Geddes) takes her turn in the window to try and talk boyfriend Robert Cosick (Richard Basehart) out of jumping

In 1959, with her career fading, Debra Paget took a strange turn performing a "snake dance" scene for a film called *The Indian Tomb*.

An actual New York street scene that helped give *Fourteen Hours* much of its immediacy

On Dangerous Ground (1951)

Combination film noir and romance story, this film stars Robert Ryan as NYC police detective Jim Wilson who's been in the trenches too long. Over the years, without a family or home life to temper his attitudes, he's become cynical about human nature and takes it out on the vermin he encounters on the job, often beating them up to get information out of them. On the edge of having to fire him, the chief of police instead sends Wilson upstate to cool off and help in a rural killing. What results is a long chase both on foot and by auto across a snow covered landscape that mirrors Wilson's hardened feelings. But when he runs into the killer's blind sister, Mary Malden (Ida Lupino), his own heart begins to melt just as the snows outside do. But in the choice between noir and romance, director Nicholas Ray and scripter A. I. Bezzerides come down firmly on the side of the angels. On the drive back to the city, Wilson has time to think and in the film's final scene, he reunites with Mary for the happy ending. Shucks! In true noir fashion, Wilson should have ignored his heart and gone back to the mean streets of the city and the lonely confines of his cheap hotel room. That said, as a romance, the film is quite effective with the viewer feeling a sense of satisfaction with its ending. Ray does a good job depicting Wilson as he moves through the two worlds with their big city hoodlums and back country hayseeds. It's all overlaid with a score by Bernard Herrmann that almost transforms the movie into a Hitchcock film with some of the music reminiscent of such pictures as *North by Northwest*. Entertaining.

Police detective Jim Wilson (Robert Ryan) expresses little patience with an underage looking barfly

150

Lupino supplied the wholesome role of Mary Malden...before going on to direct some classic noir films herself!

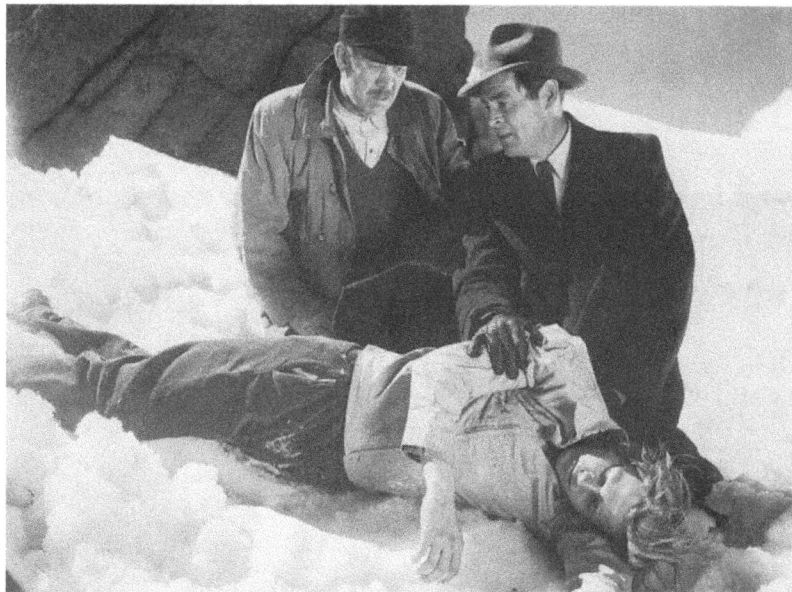

Death on the slopes: The frozen countryside was a familiar setting for many a film noir

The Sniper (1952)

Eddie Miller (Arthur Franz) hates women, or so we are told. Certainly near the start of *The Sniper,* there's a hint that as a child, Eddie may have been abused by his mother. Add to that, his experiences with women as vain, two faced, and cruel, he can't help but conclude that they cannot be trusted. A feeling of resentment that builds and builds until it explodes in violence. And as we pick up Eddie's life at the start of the film, he's just been released from an asylum. But whatever treatment he was given, didn't stick. He feels the old need to lash out and so, deliberately burns his hand as a cry for help. But doctors at the clinic he goes to don't recognize the signs and let him go. Now primed for violence, Eddie meets Jean Darr (noirette Marie Windsor) on his route as a dry cleaning delivery man. She apparently comes on to him. He reacts positively. Then she lowers the boom: she was just being sociable because she already has a boyfriend. Grrr! Next thing you know, Eddie is lying in wait for her outside the nightclub where she works. He's got a rifle in his hands. He shoots. And now the police are called in to investigate the murder. From there, the film turns into a police procedural as detective Frank Kafka (!) (Adolphe Menjou) consults with psychiatrist Dr. James Kent (noir regular Richard Kiley) who says police can't track Eddie down in the same way they do other criminals. Making the case for early identification and treatment of sex criminals, Kiley implores city authorities to take a more modern approach to the problem. In the meantime, Eddie continues to kill while writing notes to the police begging them to stop him. He's finally cornered in his apartment in a twist for film noir: no final shootout. Just Eddie sitting there looking exhausted. Directed by Edward Dmytryk and shot in harsh tones by Burnett Guffey, *The Sniper* moves right along the suspense building in tandem with Eddie being slighted by his female boss and a barfly who ends up rejecting him the latter of which becomes one of his victims. The film's most memorable scene occurs near the end when Eddie is spotted by a worker high up on the side of a smokestack. His forlorn cries warning Eddie's potential targets on the street below draw the killer's attention who then shoots him, leaving him dangling in his harness. Liberal use of San Francisco locations such as Telegraph Hill enhance the realism.

Inept ladies' man Eddie Miller (Arthur Franz) is taken in by the sociable charms of Jean Darr (Marie Windsor)

It's all in his head: Dr. James Kent (Richard Kiley) tries to explain to Det. Frank Kafka the modern method of using psychiatry in order to profile a sex killer

Eddie Miller takes aim at the hapless steeplejack who gave warning to his intended target

The Narrow Margin (1952)

Plenty of movies have been made with all the action taking place aboard a moving train with characters squeezing through tight passages from sleeping cars to dining cars etc. But none as efficiently or as excitingly done as director Richard Fleischer's *Narrow Margin*! Helping put it over the top is a great cast headed by no nonsense Charles McGraw (as Det. Walter Brown) assigned to bodyguard the wife of a mobster headed to Los Angeles to testify in court. But therein lies the rub: the woman Brown risks his life to protect (Marie Windsor) is actually an undercover policewoman. And though Windsor's performance is as tightly wound as a Swiss watch, it may have been a little too convincing for the role she's actually playing. Unknown to Brown however, the real Frankie Neall (Jacqueline White) is the pretty, blond mother of a young boy apparently traveling on her own. Fleischer performs an excellent balancing act between Brown's jousting with a crew of underworld killers aboard the train and inadvertantly making Frankie's acquaintance to the point where they'll obviously become an item once she's out of danger. But that danger is always present as the viewer is reminded by reflections in the train's windows of a car full of mobsters speeding along outside. And in a neat reversal, it's another reflection of Neall being held at gunpoint that enables Brown to pinpoint her location in a locked cabin enough to enable him to burst in and shoot the mobster before he can react. Fleischer adds to the suspense by avoiding soundtrack music. Instead, he substitutes the sounds of the train as it speeds along the tracks. It's particularly noticeable from the very start when the credits are flashed against a speeding train with only the sounds of its passage to be heard. The screenplay by Earl Felton is flawless. When talking with his partner about the sort of woman who'd marry a mobster, Brown describes the kind as "cheap, flashy, strictly poison under the gravy!" Brown would be dead wrong and lose a bet with his partner, a partner who was killed before he had a chance to collect. Adding to Brown's emotional turmoil as a result, Felton also includes a sub-text of deceit as Brown learns that part of the reason for the use of an undercover policewoman was to test him to find out if he was corrupt. At a tight 70 minute running time, there's no fat in *The Narrow Margin* only constant, full speed ahead entertainment!

Early scene from *Narrow Margin* as Det. Walter Brown (Charles McGraw) and his partner investigate a call. But only death is waiting at the top of the stairs

"Cheap, flashy, strictly poison under the gravy!" Wrong! Det. Walter Brown could not have been farther from the truth regarding Jacqueline White's Frankie Neall

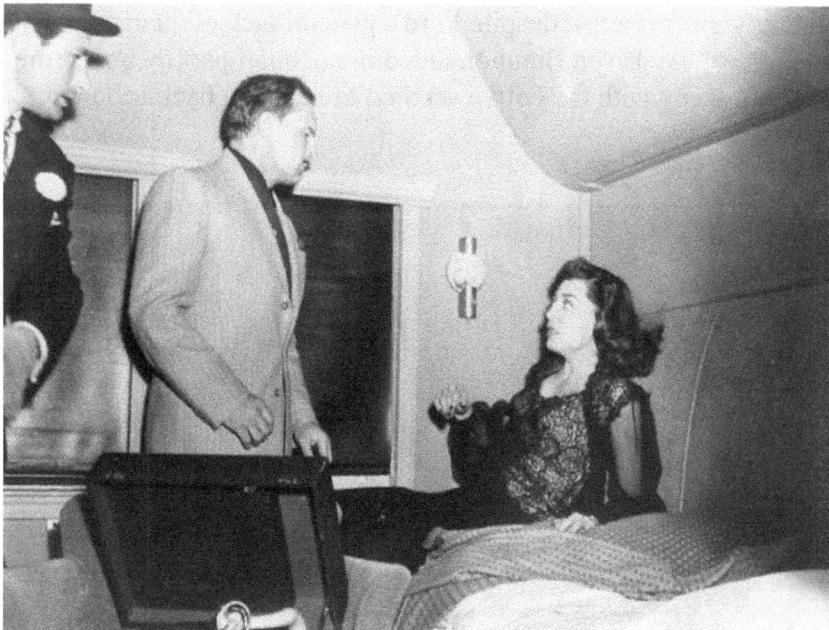

Mobsters looking for Frankie Neall think they've found her in Marie Windsor...to her extreme regret

The Big Heat (1953)

The Big Heat opens with a scene that can't be beat: a man committing suicide! From there, the film only goes from one memorable scene to another as intense Glenn Ford (detective Dave Bannion) wages a one man battle against the organized crime that controls his city. The convoluted plot begins with the aforementioned suicide of corrupt cop Tom Duncan who unbeknownst to viewers, has left behind a confession that could expose city officials' cooperation with crime lord Mike Lagana. Bannion is assigned to the case. He gets a tip from Duncan's mistress that not all was on the up and up in the Duncan household and soon after, the woman is found murdered. His suspicions fully aroused, Bannion confronts Bertha Duncan about her husband's death. In an effort to kick start his investigation, Bannion confronts Lagana and manages to rattle him. Consequently, in one of the film's most memorable sequences, one that breaks the film wide open, he receives a threatening phone call at his home and refusing to abandon the case, his wife is killed when she tries to use his car to go somewhere. Angered and unable to get anywhere within the department, Bannion resigns and goes rogue. Soon after, Bannion becomes involved with Debby Marsh (played by Gloria Graham), girlfriend of psychotic hitman Vince Stone (Lee Marvin). A bad move on Debby's part that leads to the film's second most remembered scene: learning of Debby's liason, Vince throws a pot of boiling hot coffee into her face, disfiguring her. Catching up to Larry Gordon, Vince's right hand man, Bannion forces him to come clean on the car bombing and the fact that Bertha is in possession of her husband's incriminating evidence. Later, Debby does Bannion a favor by killing Bertha herself thus causing the information to be made public. Debby follows that up by confronting Vince and turning the tables on him: she throws coffee into *his* face! Just then, Bannion busts in and a fight ensues ending with Vince's capture by police. But their arrival is too late to help Debby who was shot by Vince. There's a happy ending of sorts as the city is cleaned up and Bannion returns to his job as detective. Whew! There's a lot to unpack here but suffice it to say director Fritz Lang and screenwriter Sydney Boehm manage to keep it all straight while holding viewer interest despite Ford's general lack of charisma. This time, though, he does a good job in the role of the driven Bannion aided in no small part by noir femme fatale Gloria Graham who's unfortunate scene with the coffee seemed to be a call back to James Cagney's grapefruit from *The Public Enemy*.

Danger ahead: Detective Dave Bannion (Glenn Ford) meets in his hotel room with gang moll Debby Marsh (Gloria Graham)

Only a nut job would throw a pot of hot coffee...or anything for that matter...into Gloria Graham's face!

As usual, Lee Marvin, as Vince Stone played the unpredictable bad boy in *The Big Heat,* leaving viewers on the edge of their seats wondering when he'd suddenly explode and do something nasty

Pick Up On South Street (1953)

Small time pickpocket Skip McCoy (Richard Widmark) unknowingly interferes with a federal sting operation when he steals a roll of microfilm from Candy (Jean Peters), girlfriend of traitor Joey (noir favorite Richard Kiley). Seems Joey is in cahoots with Red agents and the feds are onto him but want to catch the ringleader so were keeping a tail on him. They go to the local police and through an informant named Moe (Thelma Ritter), they identify Skip as the pickpocket. In the meantime, Joey is upset with Candy for losing the film and tells her to get it back. Candy finds her way to Moe who tells her where to find Skip. Searching Skip's dockyard digs, Candy is taken by surprise and knocked unconscious by the pickpocket. By that point, Skip is beginning to realize the film could be worth a lot of money so that when Candy wakes upand puts the moves on him, he refuses to budge. While this is going on his Red masters put the squeeze on Joey expecting him to kill Skip to get the film back. Desperate, Joey ends up killing Moe after she refuses to tell him where to find Skip. Candy, now in love with Skip but dismayed that he still wants to deal with Joey, conks him out with a bottle and relieves him of the film then goes to the police with her story. They ask her to go back to Joey and give him the film so that he can lead them to the ringleader. She does, but Joey suspects something's up and shoots Candy leaving her for dead. His mistake. Skip hears about Candy and after seeing her in the hospital, tracks down Joey and gives him the beating of his life. Unlike the classic film noir formula, the film has a happy ending with Skip and Candy going off into the sunset with the suggestion that they will be leaving their lives of crime behind. A fast paced story slowed only slightly by romance, B film director Sam Fuller keeps things from spinning out of control (he scripted the movie too) while cinematography by Joseph MacDonald provides crisp atmosphere. Widmark is as good as he always is as venal, self-centered crook. Jean Peters is too good for him.

Stool pigeon Moe (Thelma Ritter) is confronted by a desperate Joey (Richard Kiley). The meeting will not end well

Jean Peters: Who wouldn't want to run off with her?

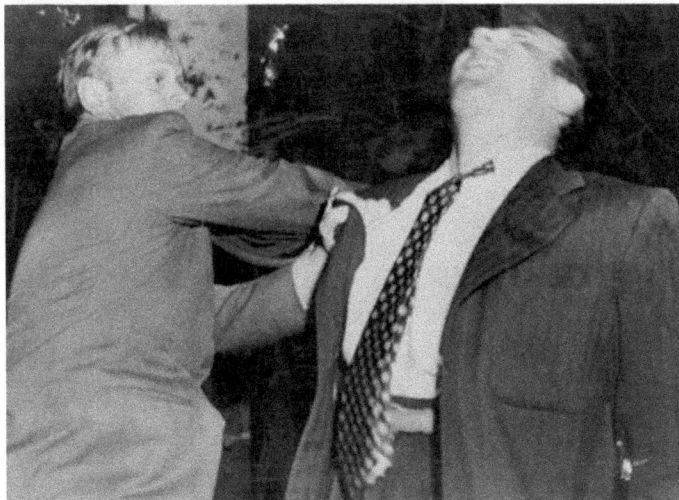

A maddened Skip McCoy gives Joey the beating of his life

Dangerous Crossing (1953)

Call this one "noir lite." Ruth Stanton (Jeanne Crain) has just married John Bowman (Carl Betz) after a whirlwind four week courtship. They board a cruise ship for their honeymoon upon which John suddenly disappears. Now Ruth is frantic trying to find him and with no evidence that he ever existed, everyone aboard thinks she's crazy. Ship's doctor Paul Manning (Michael Rennie) is assigned to keep tabs on her and in the process, begins to fall for her. Luckily, it turns out John isn't who he professed to be but someone in line to inherit Ruth's fortune if she dies. Instead, he does, clearing the way for Manning. There are a lot of red herrings thrown at the viewer here in a rather standard plot involving the only person who knows someone is missing and everyone else thinking they're out of their minds. But it works here as light entertainment keeping the viewer engaged. Direction by Joseph Newman is satisfactory with shipboard sets left over from the studio's earlier film about the Titanic. The only really noirish thing about the story is Ruth's bad move in marrying the untrustworthy John in the first place. Jeanne Crain is attractive as the flustered bride and Michael Rennie is his usual stiff, but reliable self. It's okay.

Ship's doctor Paul Manning (Michael Rennie) gets lucky putting the moves on Ruth Stanton (Jeanne Crain)

Ruth tries to explain but no one believes her

Yes, we'd believe anything Jeanne Crain told us!

Later, director Joseph Newman would contrive a clever shot of Ruth (Jeanne Crain) reflected in a porthole window: Existing sets used for the studio's expensive Titanic film were repurposed for the far less costly *Dangerous Crossing*

161

The Hitch-Hiker (1953)

At a spare 70 minutes, *The Hitch-Hiker* is as economical and tightly plotted as one could wish for in a film noir with a simple story of two men on a fishing trip to Mexico deciding to pick up a hitchhiker and learning to regret it. The two men are Roy Collins and Gilbert Bowen (Edmond O'Brien and Frank Lovejoy respectively) and the hitchhiker is one Emmett Myers (played by William Talman in one of the most manic performances ever by a noir heavy). Seems Myers is a serial killer, having murdered a number of people with whom he's already caught rides with. He allows Collins and Bowen to live primarily as protective coloration against the law that's looking for a single man in a leather jacket. Although the two men try different tactics to get away from sabotaging their car to leaving clues behind, none of it works with Myers left with the last laugh as he mocks their basic decency. Casting of Talman as the maniacal Myers was inspired. With skillful makeup that accentuates a lazy glass eye that never shuts, the actor is totally convincing as a homicidal maniac and director Ida Lupino does a wonderful job keeping his identity hidden until the moment, in the back seat of the two men's car, he comes forward out of the darkness into a key light exposing his haggard face to the viewer. One of the creepiest moments of the film takes place when the three camp out after dark. Collins and Bowen are prisoners, wrapped in their blankets like twin cocoons and separated from Myers by a trickling stream. Punctuated by close ups of his captives' frightened faces, Myers tells them about his glass eye warning them not to try to escape because they'll never know if he's asleep or not. On another night, Collins and Bowen make a break for it only to be nearly run down by Myers who pursues them in their own car. The two men fall into a protective crouch as a pair of headlights grow larger and larger. They fully expect to be run over by the homicidal Myers. But at the last minute, the car stops short. Myers steps out not to shoot them, but to taunt them, continuing to play his mind games with them. Through the various incidents in their journey, one that takes place against a pitiless desert landscape, Collins and Gilbert gradually lose heart as well as their strength until by the end, they're ill shaven, dirty, and staggering while Myers still seems fresh and upbeat. They and the audience have no reason to expect anything but death after the killer has no more need for them. Lupino also worked on the screenplay with producer/husband Collier Young, basing the story on actual events. One of the true classics of film noir, *The Hitch-Hiker* is a must see by any fan!

On location for *The Hitchhiker*, director Ida Lupino talks to stars Edmond O'Brien and Frank Lovejoy

Roy Collins and Gilbert Bowen (Edmond O'Brien and Frank Lovejoy) suddenly find themselves at the mercy of serial killer Emmett Myers (William Talman) in a scene just before Talman leans forward into a key light

William Talman as Emmett Myers keeps a sleepy glass eye on his captives

Human Desire (1954)

Love and death among the train yards of the Rock Island Railroad located in El Reno, Oklahoma. That's where dull Glenn Ford (as returning vet Jeff Warren) finds vivacious Vicki Buckley (Gloria Graham) married to old acquaintance and insanely jealous Carl Buckley (Broderick Crawford). But it seems that Carl has been fired and convinces his wife to take advantage of her former acquaintance with railroad boss John Owens to give him his job back. She succeeds, but now Carl wonders what she had to do to win Owens over. In a rage, he forces Vickie to write a note to Owens asking him to meet her on the train back home. On the train, Carl kills Owens and retrieves the letter holding it as blackmail against Vicki ever leaving him. But as they ready themselves to leave the train compartment, Carl spots Jeff and gets Vicki to distract him while he slips away. Jeff goes all sweet over Vicki and when an inquest is made on the murder of Owens, he makes his big mistake but lying about Vicki's presence on the train. Later, Jeff compounds his mistake by falling hard for Vicki and after learning of Carl's hold over her, plots to kill him and get the letter back. But at the last minute, Jeff comes to his senses and returns to Vicki confronting her with the realization that she's been playing him for a fool. Of course! Jeff, Jeff! Get with the program! Later, Carl returns to Vicki imploring her to stay even without the letter that Jeff had yet retrieved from the drunken Carl. She refuses and ends up being strangled to death for her trouble. Meanwhile, Jeff, now back in his right mind, goes back to good girl Ellen (Kathleen Case) who'd been waiting in the wings for him all the time. Despite its origins in a French film, *Human Desire* rises above its source material to make for an interesting movie. Shot on location in actual train yards, it retains a gritty realism essential in making the story of love and murder believable. Ford transcends, just barely, his innate dullness and Graham is very good as the conniving Vickie. Another mini-triumph for director Fritz Lang and cinematographer Burnett Guffey. More than worth a look.

Location shooting at the Rock Island Railroad located in El Reno, Oklahoma was a key element in establishing the credibility of *Human Desire*

It was no wonder that Gloria Graham was often cast as a noir femme fatale; she was often deadly to the male of species!

Danger ahead: With her bed in the background, the unsuspecting Jeff Warren (Glenn Ford) is oh so easily lured into Vicki's honey trap!

Pushover (1954)

Fred McMurray is L.A. Detective Paul Sheridan who makes the mistake of falling for the woman he's been assigned to keep tabs on. Before he knows it, he's in deep, too deep! Seems Sheridan took his job too seriously and moved in on Lona McLane (Kim Novak), the girlfriend of mobster Harry Wheeler whom the cops are looking for after he robbed a bank of $200,000. Part of a team keeping watch on McLane's apartment, Sheridan continues to meet with her on the sly. Together, they plot to grab the stolen cash for themselves and take off for parts unknown. Sheridan develops an elaborate plan to get hold of the money but it falls apart when a fellow cop gets suspicious and he's forced to do him in. Adding to this is McLane's pretty neighbor, Ann Stewart (Dorothy Malone), who catches Sheridan in McLane's apartment when she goes over to borrow some sugar. Later, she recognizes him and suspects him as being Wheeler. In the meantime, Ann has become attracted to Sheridan's partner, Phil Carey (Rick McAllister). The feeling's mutual. When she points out the man she saw in the apartment, the game is up for Sheridan who makes a break for it and is shot by his fellow policemen for his pains. Following the classic noir formula, *Pushover* is just perfect in every respect including its location shooting with a fabulous establishing shot of the Los Angeles City Hall at the start. Director Richard Quine does an excellent job for this low budget thriller while cinematographer Lester White shows a mastery of moody shadow. Of course, noir favorite Fred McMurray is in his element as Paul Sheridan (despite the film's slim resemblance to his earlier *Double Indemnity*). Nobody could depict a struggle of conscience the way MacMurray does in those solitary shots as he broods, puffing on a cigarette. And though others might rave over Kim Novak's appearance here, it's Dorothy Malone that steals hearts. Highly recommended.

Detective Paul Sheridan (Fred MacMurray) finds himself a *Pushover* for mob moll Lona McLane (Kim Novak)

On the other hand, Sheridan's partner, Phil Carey (Rick McAllister) may have hit the real jackpot with Dorothy Malone's Ann Stewart. She can borrow a cup of sugar from us anytime!

Under certain circumstances, it's perfectly understandable that Paul Sheridan could fall for Kim Novak's Lona McLane.

On the Waterfront (1954)

Might be considered more of a crime film than film noir but Terry Malloy's (Marlon Brando) early decisions first to throw a key boxing match and then allowing himself to be used by the mob that controls the waterfront as a "pigeon" for the murder of a government witness can be seen to fit the noir mold. Brando is unforgettable in the role of the somewhat dumb Malloy whose older brother (Rod Steiger) is an attorney for mob boss Johnny Friendly (Lee J. Cobb). But after he realizes that he's been a tool of Friendly for years and then falls in love with Edie Doyle (Eva Marie Saint), the sister of the man he set up for murder, Terry develops a conscience that sets him in opposition to the mob. Saint, in her debut role is waiflike, tender and strong when needed and a convincing female figure who could win Malloy over and give him the courage to stand up for what's right. Meanwhile, Cobb is absolutely menacing as the "friendly" Friendly when it suits his purpose and ruthlessly scary when it doesn't. His hand to hand fight with Terry at the film's conclusion is brutal and leaves Terry badly beaten. Not to be outdone too is Karl Malden as Father Barry, the fighting priest determined to break the mob's hold on the docks. Director Elia Kazan wastes no time bringing the viewer up to speed with an opening shot that contrasts the non-descript shack that's headquarters for the mob and the huge, stately ocean liner in the background. Contrary to expectations, all the power in the scene lies in that shack, not with the ivory tower owners of the liner. Meanwhile, that same shot sets up a key scene in which Terry and a line of gangsters leaves the shack on their way to throw the hapless Joey Doyle from the roof of his tenement building. Kazan's direction throughout this masterpiece is flawless with every scene watchable and interesting. Shot entirely on location in Hoboken, New Jersey, he fills every shot of empty playgrounds, dark alleys, rooftops, and cold dockyards with a low lying mist in the daytime and slick, rain soaked streets at night. Many shots include rail yards and trash heaps bounded by chain link fences in the foreground while the majestic spires of New York skyscrapers loom across the oil slick river that also separates two vastly different worlds. Chalk up most of that visual magic to cinematographer Boris Kaufman who paints everything in a dreary black and white that completely captures the Hoboken neighborhoods' atmosphere of despair and desperation. Finally, screenwriter Budd Schulberg, besides providing the film with its most unforgettable line ("I coulda been a contender," Terry tells his brother. "I coulda been somebody instead of a bum, which is what I am.") presents viewers with a nice metaphor that compares Terry's pigeons and the hawks that prey on them to the cowed dock workers and the gangsters who exploit them. Schulberg did a ton of research before writing the script including talking to the real life principles Anthony DeVincenzo and Fr. John Corridon involved with breaking the mob's hold on the longshoremen's union. Filled with one dramatic moment after another (Fr. Barry's speech in the hold of the ship; Terry's discovery of his brother's body; Terry putting on Edie's glove while talking with her in the park, etc) with great performances by a great cast, this one should be first on anyone's must see list!

Key scene as Edie Doyle (Eva Marie Saint) touches Terry's conscience

In a powerful scene, Karl Malden as Father Barry speaks out against the mob's hold on the union from the hold of a ship and gets hit with rotten vegetables for his trouble

Terry Maloy (Marlon Brando) will defy the mob and help break their hold on the docks

Crime Wave (1954)

In *Crime Wave,* the viewer is thrown immediately into the action as the film opens with a small time robbery of a gas station. Within seconds, the operator is knocked unconscious, a passing policeman is killed, and one of the gang wounded, and dropped off with some of the take to find his way to the apartment of ex-con Steve Lacey (Gene Nelson). Now happily married and holding down a job as an airplane mechanic, Steve can't escape his past when the wounded crook shows up in his living room and promptly kicks the bucket. That's when Steve reaches his noir decision point: instead of calling the police immediately as wife Ellen advises (Phyllis Kirk), he hesitates and calls his parole officer instead. Thus, when the cops arrive led by the cynical Det. Sims (Sterling Hayden), he's forced into a corner with the prospect of losing everything he's gained since leaving prison. Luckily, the parole officer gets him off but back at his apartment, the remaining two crooks muscle in and threaten Ellen unless Steve cooperates in their plan to rob a bank. When he reluctantly agrees, he finds out that not only will he drive the getaway car but fly the getaway plane as well! A complicating factor is disbarred medico Doc Penny (Ted de Corsia) whom the dead crook had asked to meet him at Steve's apartment. Suspecting his reliability, Ben Hastings (Charles Bronson) is detailed to keep an eye on him. Instead, he murders him. While Nelson is good as the ex-con trying to go straight and Kirk is believable as she goes from standing by her man to being vulnerable in clutches of lascivious bad boy Johnny Haslett, it's Hayden that steals the show with his hard bitten, seen it all, depiction of Detective Sims. With his lean frame carelessly sprawled in a swivel chair either at his office or elsewhere and gnawing on a toothpick, his rapid fire accusations and denunciations are shot with machine gun rapidity at targets like Steve Lacey as if they were a fish in a barrel. Director Andre de Toth takes full advantage of location work around nighted Los Angeles streets with that of the opening shots of the gas station and the building where Ellen Tracey is held being the gritty standouts. With cinematographer Bert Glennon capturing the location shoots in all their stark realism, *Crime Wave* adds up to a perfect little noir nugget!

The gas station location where all the action in *Crimewave* is kicked off

With his lanky frame and world weary attitude, Sterling Hayden was perfect casting as the cynical Det. Sims

Phyllis Kirk's Ellen Lacy gave husband Steve plenty of reason to beat the rap being hung on him and prove his innocence!

Drive a Crooked Road (1954)

Mickey Rooney does it again! After his film noir classic *Quicksand*, shot in 1950, Rooney returned to the genre in a followup classic called *Drive a Crooked Road* (love that title!) In it, he plays hapless auto mechanic and sometimes race car driver Eddie Shannon. Lonely and kidded by his fellow garage workers because of his dimunative height, he's the perfect mark for femme fatale Barbara Matthews (Dianne Foster). Falling hard for Barbara's sultry charms, Eddie is talked into driving the getaway car for a bank heist brainstormed by Steve Norris (Kevin McCarthy) who's Barbara's actual squeeze. Norris needs Eddie's driving skills in order to take the getaway car down a particular stretch of bad roadway in time to head off road blocks sure to be set up by the police. But as with most noir films, things go south and the truth of Barbara's deception comes out. And although Barbara suffers the pangs of conscience, they aren't enough to save either herself or Eddie from the ultimate consequences of their choices. A perfect noir that fulfills the classic formula following the "crooked road" to its ultimate and logical end, this film can't be beat! Direction by Richard Quine with much location work is good even though cinematography by Charles Lawton is mostly lacking. But then, the film's stark realism perhaps needed little artificially induced atmosphere to put across Blake Edwards' fast moving script. Rooney, following a difficult period adjusting from successful ingenue to unwanted adult star, seemed to find his niche in the noir genre and McCarthy is smooth and affable as the cold blooded Steve Norris. Of course, it goes without saying that the beautiful Foster would have no trouble at all making even the hardest case of women hater fall for her obvious charms! A must see.

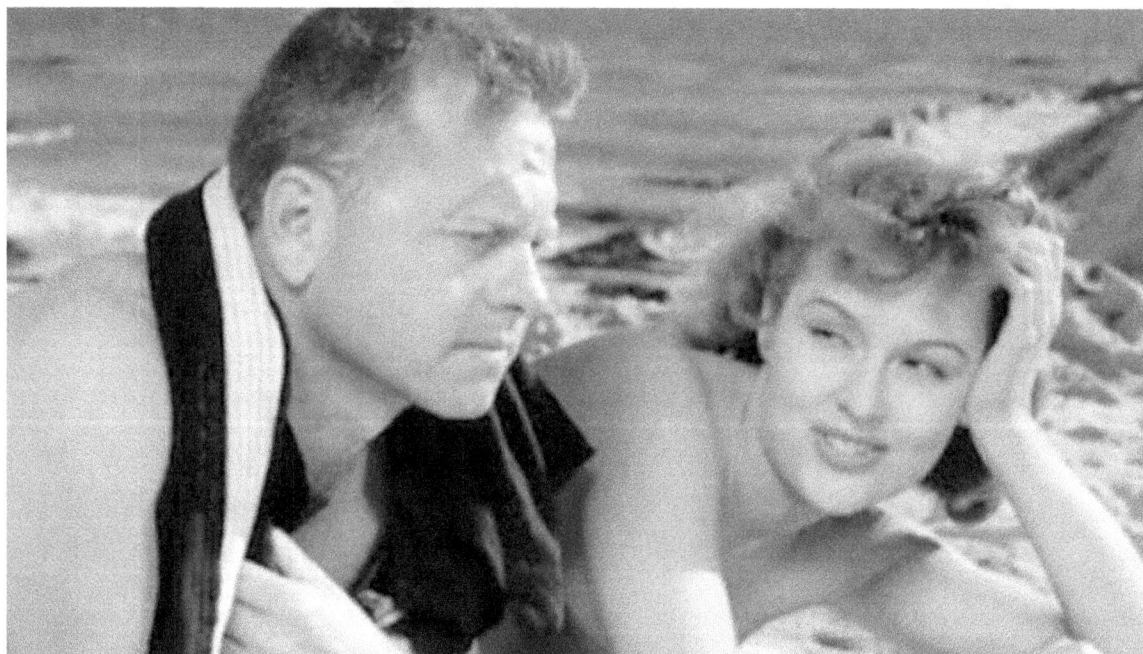

Watch it Eddie! Eddie Shannon (Mickey Rooney) is expertly had by the sultry Barbara Matthews (Dianne Foster).

An older Mickey Rooney successfully transitioned from ingenue roles to film noir usually playing the part of a fall guy

Eddie Shannon (Mickey Rooney) drives the getaway car while mastermind Steve Norris (Kevin McCarthy) rides shotgun

Kiss Me Deadly (1955)

Director Robert Aldrich launches the viewer right into the action with a woman running down a lonely, nighted highway dressed in nothing but a stolen coat. After risking her life to force him to the side of the road, she's picked up by sleazy divorce dick Mike Hammer (Ralph Meeker). From there, the credits begin to roll but instead of a film score, only the sound of the woman's out of breath panting is heard over the car's engine noise. Mike lies his way through a roadblock set up to capture the woman (who claims she was unjustly held in an asylum) only to be captured by a gang of hoodlums who proceed to torture the woman to death before driving her body along with Mike over a cliff to his own apparent death. Whew! And that's just the opening ten minutes of this mystery thriller based on the novel by Mickey Spillane, a former men's sweat hack whose signature character, Mike Hammer, is hard boiled to the point of caricature. For that, Meeker is perfect with a face that rarely registers emotion even when friends are being murdered, his "secretary" and lover is trying to get a rise out of him, or when his own life is being threatened. But somehow it all works as Mike threads his way among gangsters, government agents, femme fatales, and his own amorous secretary in the form of Velda (played by a sultry Maxine Cooper) to acquire the "great whatsit" that everyone is trying to find. What it is is a piece of nuclear material. But Mike doesn't know that. Tired of his regular nickel and dime operations setting up cheating spouses in blackmail schemes (for which he cynically employs Velda's charms for entrapment purposes), he thinks there's real money to be had in horning in on the whatsit game. There is, but a slob like him isn't going get any of it. Not if evil mastermind Dr. Soberin (Albert Dekker) has anything to say about it. Wonderfully directed, Aldrich takes his time to tell the complicated story made up of many small highlights including a police grilling that really tars and feathers Mike's sleazy operations; a scene in a bathhouse where off camera, Mike takes out a hoodlum in such a way that it frightens the guy's partner; the crushing of a mechanic when a hoodlum releases the hold on the jack holding up the car he's working under; Mike's breaking of the fingers of a morgue attendant who's being uncooperative; and of course, the spectacular finish. All made even more urgent with location shooting in the Bunker Hill district of Los Angeles. As for the sensational script, writer Al Bezerrides luckily didn't stick much to the novel and likely only improved on it despite Spillane's disapproval. In all respects, despite its source material, *Kiss Me Deadly* is a top notch mystery thriller and perhaps, one of the blackest of noirs in its disregard of human life, human emotions, and its nihilistic "hero" who, as the woman he picks up at the beginning of the film says "you're not a giver, you'll always take."

A shot from the unforgettable opening scenes of *Kiss Me Deadly* as Mike Hammer comes across a woman wearing only an overcoat

Deadly dame: The childlike personality of Lily Carver (Gaby Rogers) was only cover for this deceitful and dangerous femme

"Secretary" Velda Wickman (Maxine Cooper) works over Mike Hammer (Ralph Meeker) who manages to keep his cool

Five Against the House (1955)

A good film with script by noir regular Stirling Siliphant that takes just a little too long to get started. It's about college buddies Al Mercer (Guy Madison), Brick (Brian Keith), Ronnie (Kerwin Mathews), and Roy (Alvy Moore) who conceive a plot to rob real life Harold's Club in Reno, Nevada. According to Ronnie, who conceives the idea, they wouldn't keep the money, it was just to see if they could succeed where others had failed. Unfortunately, loose cannon Brick has other ideas. Brick, played by Brian Keith is the standout of *Five Against the House* as a Korean War veteran suffering from PTSD. When he loses control in a fight against another student, the audience believes him. Nevertheless, they also want to like him. Keith had that quality allowing him to play nice guys and bad guys both with equal dexterity with his bad guy personas often being the quiet time bombs who could blow up at any minute. That said, despite some speed bumps involving campus hi-jinks with a pre-*Green Acres* Alvy Moore supplying the humor and romantic interludes between Al and Kaye Greylek (Kim Novak), once the actual heist begins, director Phil Karlson inserts a measure of suspense that builds toward the climax and expected confrontation between Al and Brick. Location shooting in Reno really helps including an automated garage sequence and Harold's Club itself.

Unlikely looking students Roy (Alvy Moore), Brick (Brian Keith), Ronnie (Kerwin Mathews), and Al (Guy Madison) watch as Kaye Greylek (Kim Novak) perform in a local night club

Kim Novak: Too much woman for a mere college student?

176

The automated garage where the climactic moments of *Five Against the House* takes place

Al and Brick, disguised as bearded cowboys, bluff William Conrad playing a house employee

Storm Fear (1955)

Slow burn noir in which gang of payroll thieves hold up in an isolated farmhouse occupied by a family whose father regards himself as a failure and who happens to be the older brother of gang leader Charlie Blake (Cornel Wilde) As a snow storm socks the group into the house preventing them from moving on, close quarters then enable viewers to learn more about the relationship between Charlie, brother Fred (Dan Duryea), wife Edna (Lee Grant), and son David (David Stollery) The slow drip drip of facts that fill in these characters' past is what keeps viewer interest pending the climactic escape wherein young David is compelled to lead the gang over a mountain to safety. A noir that falls into the sub-category of innocent group of people held hostage by bad guys, this one is better than most with Wilde not only starring, but producing and directing as well. Location shooting in California's Sun Valley is fine as is most of the cast. Stollery is excellent as the wide eyed kid forced to lead the gang over the mountain and Stephen Hill is good too as the at once childlike but psychotic Benjie. Duryea, in a different kind of part for him, is solid in the dispirited role as down and out Fred living off the stolen handouts of younger brother Charlie while also married to his ex-girlfriend. Lee Grant as Edna passes muster but there's something about her delivery that rings false. Watch for Dennis Weaver in a small but important role as the hired hand with the eye for Edna. Interestingly, the novel upon which the movie is based was told from the point of view of twelve year old David of which some sense is retained in the film.

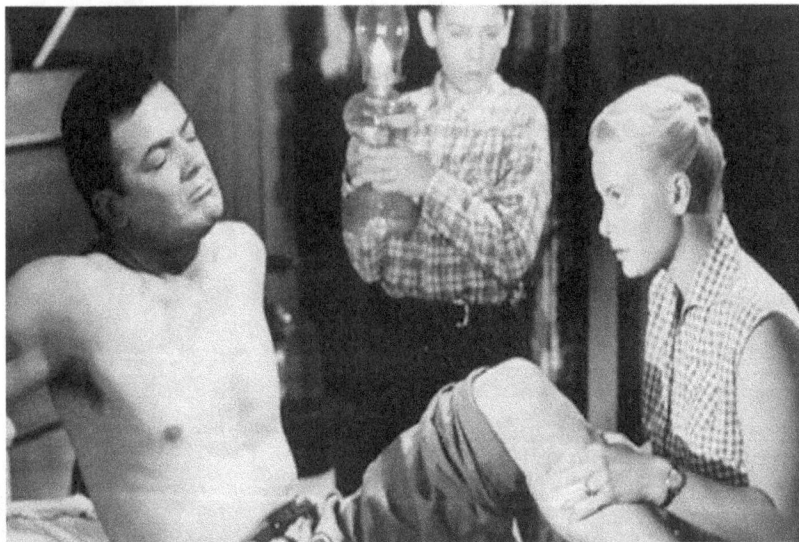

Exploration of conflicting characterizations is the order of the day in *Storm Fear* as a wounded Charlie Blake (Cornel Wilde) is ministered by ex girlfriend and currently his brother's wife Edna Blake (Lee Grant) while a wary David Blake (David Stollery) (who could be Charlie's own son) looks on

Storm Fear's wild card is Stephen Hill as the volatile Benjie

Bank robbers on the lam: Besides leader Charlie Blake and psycho henchman Benjie, the group also included Charlie's current squeeze, Elizabeth, destined for a dismal fate at the climax to *Storm Fear*

Phenix City Story (1955)

A hard boiled and hard hitting tale of a small Alabama town treed for over 100 years by the mob, Phenix City Story is told in semi-documentary style opening with a longish sequence designed to seem like an extended news program reporting in the aftermath of the events to be detailed once the film proper begins. Location shooting by director Phil Karlson gives the story, based on actual events, versimilitude. A character in itself, is the night club where most of the overt illicit action occurs and where the resistance against the law is concocted. As the film proper begins, young military officer and family man John Patterson (Richard Kiley) arrives in town and is quickly swept up in its illegal activity after he breaks up a beating by thugs of a group of crusading citizens. Up to now, Patterson's attorney father, Albert (John McIntyre), has played a neutral game but after the beating and with his son's prompting, agrees to run for attorney general promising to clean up the city. The mob is aroused and through intimidation tactics (such as a horrifying scene in which a Black child is murdered and her body thrown from a car onto the Patterson's front lawn) and its control of local police and politicians, attempts to thwart Patterson's election. Finally, as in the real life events upon which the film is based, the candidate is murdered after which John Patterson replaces his father on the ticket. After a rousing speech against the mob and despite massive election interference, he wins the election. In real life, martial law was declared after the death of Albert Patterson and Phenix City is finally cleaned up. The film's low budget actually works in the film's favor, giving it a raw edge in tune with the small town seediness of the goings on especially when the viewer is taken inside the town's night club. Far from the glitzy Hollywood versions of its New York counterparts, the Poppy Club is all bare floorboards and peeling wallpaper. Claustrophobic back rooms with battered furniture is where corpulent and sweaty Edward Andrews as mob chieftan Rhett Tanner holds court. There, he schemes to rip off off duty soldiers from the nearby army base while presenting a friendly front to local citizens. The club floor is crowded and smoke filled with local floozies holding down gambling tables while a sultry chanteuse weaves among the tables. *Phenix City Story* is as far removed from fifties complacency and normalcy as one could imagine.

A local citizen of Phenix City is fed up with the goings on in the Poppy Club, but alone and unaided, his protest can only end badly

Location shooting went a long way in giving *The Phenix City Story* its, grimy, realistic feel

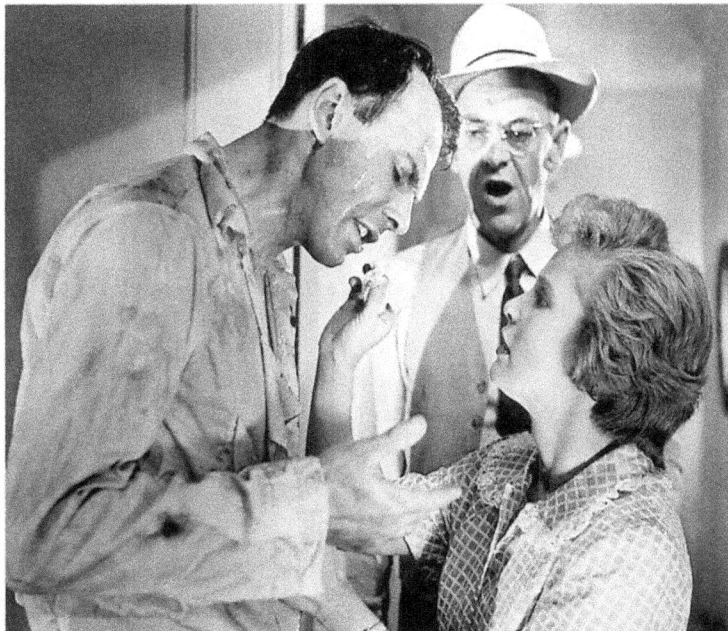

After his son, John Patterson (Richard Kiley), is beaten up by the mob, Albert Patterson (John McIntyre) decides to run for attorney general vowing to clean up Phenix City

Bad Day at Black Rock (1955)

Spencer Tracey is John Macreedy, a wounded veteran who lost an arm in Italy who suddenly appears in the isolated desert town of Black Rock. So rarely does the train ever stop at the cluster of ramshackle buildings that his arrival causes an immediate stir as local residents give him the eye or turn a cold shoulder whenever he asks a question. A borderline noir, *Bad Day at Black Rock*, as adapted from a short story by screenwriters Don McGuire and Millard Kaufman, is a tight murder mystery whose suspense begins to mount as soon as Macreedy steps off the train. In Black Rock, he's confronted by a constellation of stars including Lee Marvin, Ernest Borgnine, Walter Brennan, Dean Jagger, Anne Francis, and Robert Ryan and director John Sturges holds viewer interest right from the start as Macreedy tries to look up the father of a man who saved his life back in Italy, one Komoko, a Japanese homesteader. But Komoko has been murdered by some of the townsfolk led by Reno Smith (Robert Ryan) whose restrained menace has cowed the rest of the community into silence. Now, they plot to kill Macreedy lest he report the murder to the authorities. Ryan is excellent as the smart and dangerous ringleader whose implied menace keeps everyone else in line. Marvin as right hand man Hector David is clearly threatening while Borgnine is perfect as town bully Coley Trimble who gets his surprising comeuppance at the hand of the one armed Macreedy. Interestingly, there had been talk of Alan Ladd being cast as Macreedy and that would have been fantastic. But the older, more ponderous Tracey does manage to fill the bill here as an unlikely looking hero. Filmed in color, the movie stands in contrast with most film noir but the actual desert locations more than make up for that. The film, with its small town with a secret theme, is interesting and holds the attention for the full length of its amazingly brief 81 minute running time. Viewers are constantly left wondering how the one armed Macreedy can escape his own murder when the whole town is against him with no contact with the outside world and with a train that won't return for him for another twenty-four hours. Excellent all around.

John Macreedy (Spencer Tracey) arrives in Black Rock and immediately encounters unwelcoming Ernest Borgnine and Lee Marvin

182

Massacre rents a jeep from female garage mechanic Liz Wirth (Ann Francis) that will draw the unwanted attention of Reno Smith

Director John Sturges and crew shoot a scene with Spencer Tracey and Robert Ryan

Tight Spot (1955)

Slow moving semi-noir featuring Brian Keith as Det. Vince Striker assigned to bodyguard mob witness Sherry Conley (an aging Ginger Rogers). Held in a hotel room, various attempts are made on Sherry's life by mob leader Benjamin Costain (Lorne Greene) whom she's scheduled to testify against. But there's the rub. Sherry absolutely refuses to testify fearing for her life. But after being in close contact with Vince through most of the film, she develops a soft spot for him. But unbeknownst to her, he's actually dirty, being an informer for the mob. But he's not immune to Sherry's charms either and in the end, he sacrifices his life for hers. Originally written as a play, it shows in the film's relatively static scenes directed by Phil Karlson with little or no location or even exterior work to liven things up a bit. Cast is good with Keith doing his usual solid job. Edward G. Robinson, on the back slope of his career, is a decided second banana here as U.S. Attorney Lloyd Hallett trying to con Sherry into testifying. Original title to the story, *Dead Pigeon* would have evoked more interest than *Tight Spot*. Shrug.

Looks like Ginger Rogers (as Sherry Conley) is in a *Tight Spot* as Det. Vince Striker (Brian Keith) checks up on her!

Things get even tighter here as Striker and Conley become emotionally involved

U.S. Attorney Lloyd Hallett (Edward G. Robinson) works over Sherry Conley trying to convince her to turn state's evidence

Ginger Rogers was past her prime by the time she was cast in *Tight Spot* but producers may have calculated that her name recognition value trumped her fitness for the role

Illegal (1955)

Not exactly a film noir, *Illegal* is fatally marred by a questionable portrayal of the legal process from start to finish. Starring Edward G. Robinson as self confident DA Victor Scott, the film opens with Scott sending an innocent man to the electric chair before finding that he was innocent after all. As a result, Scott hits the skids, becomes an alcoholic and ends up in the drunk tank. Eventually, he rises above it and through sketchy legal tactics finds success as a defense attorney. From there, he becomes involved with gangster Frank Garland (Albert Dekker) and only breaks free when he's forced to choose between Dekker and Ellen Miles (Nina Foch) who's been accused of murder and whom he's raised as his own daughter. Fearing exposure, Garland has Scott shot but before he collapses in death, Scott manages one last trick proving Ellen's innocence and Garland's guilt. Unimaginatively directed by Lewis Allen and straightforwardly shot by one J. Peverell Marley, the film lacks any atmosphere traditional to noir and is filmed mostly on a backlot. It's not aided by the W.R. Burnett and James Webb script. The two most assuredly, did no legal research before writing the screenplay! Throughout, the film's believability is held back by legal maneuvers that no one would ever get away with in real life as well as what should have been an open and shut case of self defense by Ellen but all exculpatory evidence is ignored both by the defense and the boob who calls himself the new DA (Edward Platt was stuck with the role) The only real notable thing to mention about the film is its list of fun co-stars including Jane Mansfield (the blond bombshell who fulfills the same role here as Marilyn Monroe did over in *Asphalt Jungle* ie bad guy plaything); Ellen Corby (who was everywhere in movies and TV before getting her big break on *The Waltons*); Hugh Marlowe; and DeForest Kelley (way before his own breakthrough role on the *Star Trek* TV show). Skippable.

A pre-*Star Trek* Deforest Kelly walks the last mile setting off the events of *Illegal*

Jane Mansfield provided the eye candy as the aptly named Angel O'Hara in *Illegal* and perhaps the only good reason for watching it

The legal shenanigans in *Illegal* are at best unlegalistic!

Night of the Hunter (1955)

Where to start on this incredible, jam packed movie where literally everything is laden with double meaning? The first and only film directed by actor Charles Laughton, *Night of the Hunter* employs the tools of silent cinema as well as foreshadowing, symbolism, and metaphor in telling its story of a false minister looking for stolen money. The film is complicated further by an overlay that inverts noir expectations this time with the wife and children suffering the consequences of a bad decision made by the husband and father. Peter Graves plays Ben Harper, the husband in question. He's arrested by police following his participation in a bank robbery but not before he hides the stolen cash. The question of the whereabouts of the money is uppermost in the mind of Harper's cellmate, faux preacherman Harry Powell (Robert Mitchum). Failing to learn the secret from Harper, Powell, still hoping to find the money, seeks out the now widowed Willa Harper and marries her hoping she was privy to her husband's secret. But as viewers discover, Willa is ignorant of the cash but not so the Harper children, John and Pearl. What follows is the sometimes sinister, often creepy attempts by Powell to coerce the children into revealing the secret culminating in his murder of Willa. From there, the children escape and embark on a surreal river journey made all the more strange by Laughton's use of artificial sets and atmospheric lighting. The children eventually alight at the farm of Rachel Cooper (Lilian Gish) a kind of modern mother goose who's been taking in stray youngsters cast adrift in the Great Depression. A film noir disguised as an art film, *Night of the Hunter* was one of the top cinematic achievements of the decade despite being little recognized as such at the time. Mitchum's role as the Rev. Powell has rightfully gone down as one of the most disturbing characters ever created for the camera with his mockery of Christianity and the words "love" and "hate" penned on the fingers of either hand. In contrast, Gish creates a Biblical, otherworldly figure that's equally iconic. Enhancing Mitchum and Gish's performances was the cinematography by Stanley Cortez who sculpted in shadows filling empty spaces and transforming others into things of beauty. A must see.

One of many iconic images from *Night of the Hunter*. Here, in a set reminiscent of a church, Harry Powell (Robert Mitchum) prepares to murder Willa

Willa's body at the bottom of the river where Harry Powell has dumped it, glowing in a heavenly light

Wonderful example of set design and Stanley Cortez' cinematography

Big House USA (1955)

Under the misleading title of *Big House USA* actually lurks an unusually cold blooded noir. The time spent behind bars during the film's brief 83 minutes comprises only the middle third of the movie. The first third spotlights Ralph Meeker as kidnapper Jerry Barker. Meeker is most often cited for the classic noir thriller *Kiss Me Deadly* but his bluff acting style is much more suited to this near forgotten film where he convincingly plays an affable hiker who finds a missing boy lost in a state park. The audience is fooled until he leaves the boy alone in an unsafe fire tower. Now revealed as a bad guy, Barker goes about squeezing the boy's father for $200,000 in ransom money. In the meantime, the boy tries to leave the fire tower and falls to his death. When Barker returns and finds his body, he coldly picks it up and tosses it into a gorge (where it's never found) Proceeding with his plan, he gets the money, but that's when the story takes an unexpected turn: he's caught and convicted for kidnapping but the money is never found and his responsibility in the boy's death is never proven. Now dubbed by the press as "the Iceman" due to his sans froid, he receives a sentence of only a few months. In jail however, he's thrown in with a bunch of hardened criminals, a rogues gallery that includes Rollo Lamar (Broderick Crawford), William "Machine Gun" Mason, (William Talman), Alamo Smith (Lon Chaney), and Benny Kelly (Charles Bronson)! Knowing that his $200,000 is still hidden in the state park somewhere, the group forces Barton to escape jail with them but once out, the ruthless Rollo kills off Alamo and Benny (right after Benny saves his life!) While all this is going on, FBI agent James Madden (Reed Hadley) has been on the case and has managed to track down Barton's accomplice (Felicia Farr as Nurse Emily Evans). Figuring that Rollo didn't help the Iceman escape from jail for his health, Madden keeps rangers at the park on alert. That's when the final third of the film kicks in. When the gang is spotted, a shootout results. A final word by Madden (who's been narrating the story all along) lets viewers know that Barton eventually got the electric chair even though his responsibility for the death of the boy was never proven. All in all, this was an exciting, fast paced, double track story. Director Howard Koch makes sure there's never a dull moment even as the film shifts from documentary style to police procedural to crime drama. Location shooting in the great outdoors as well as in an actual prison setting adds versimilitude to the proceedings. Meeker's performance as the Iceman is the standout but Crawford is suitably ruthless and Talman by turns a dangerous or reluctant killer. See it.

A true rogues' gallery: Inmates Benny Kelly (Charles Bronson), William "Machine Gun" Mason, (William Talman), Alamo Smith (Lon Chaney), and Rollo Lamar (Broderick Crawford)

Fatal encounter: "Iceman" Jerry Barker (Ralph Meeker) finds a missing boy instructing him to remain in an old fire tower while he goes for help. Meeker's cold blooded portrayal of Barker is one for the books

Kittenish Felicia Farr played nurse for Ralph Meeker's Jerry Barker but even she couldn't thaw the "iceman!"

The Killing (1956)

The perfect heist movie moves like clockwork as Stanley Kubrick directs his first film. And it's a doozy! Sterling Heyden is two time loser Johnny Clay with a can't lose plan to rob a racetrack. To do it, he brings in a group of key people who'll share in the moulah when the job is complete: Marvin Unger (Jay C. Flippen, has a soft spot for Clay and provides the seed money); Randy Kennon (Ted de Corsia, a corrupt cop); Mike O'Reilly (Joe Sawyer with a sick wife); and George Peatty (a nebbish with a greedy wife played by Elisha Cook Jr). Ancillary to the plan but with no need to know more than their parts include Maurice (a chess loving pro wrestler played by Kola Kwariani) and Nicky Arane (Timothy Carey as a sharpshooter hired to murder a horse!) But there's a fly in the ointment in the form of Peatty's grasping wife, Sherry (Marie Windsor) who's cheating on her desperate to please husband. The darkly handsome Val Cannon is the cuckold (noir favorite Vince Edwards) who breaks in on the gang after they've successfully robbed the racetrack to steal the swag for himself. But shooting erupts and everyone except George is killed. While the wounded George goes back to his wife to exact rough justice, Clay shows up and, seeing trouble, takes off with the cash and long suffering girlfriend Fay (Coleen Gray). He makes it to the airport to catch their flight but a faulty suitcase in which he stuffed the money bursts while being transported to the plane. The money ends up scattered all over the airport by the backdraft of a plane's props. Kubrik does such a fine job telling this tale from the point of view of the crooks that the viewer ends up sympathizing with them and hoping that they succeed in their wild plan. A great cast is headed by Heyden whose clipped but nuanced performance handily wins over the viewer. Cook is marvelous as the mousy George Peatty groveling at every cutting remark from his wife. The film itself is constructed in a novel way telling its story using both flashbacks and flash forwards forming a jigsaw puzzle that all comes together in the end. Not to be missed!

Iconic moment when a disguised Johnny Clay (Sterling Heyden) breaks in on the purser to rob the racetrack

Val Cannon (Vince Edwards) breaks up the party

Colleen Grey, as Fay, distracts the eye in an otherwise bleak, no-nonsense story

The Burglar (1957)

A neat character study as well as heist gone wrong noir, *The Burglar* is Dan Duryea as Nat Harbin who heads a trio of helpers including a pair of low grade thugs and beautiful Gladden played by Jane Mansfield in her breakthrough role. Nat manages to burgle a diamond necklace but in doing so, is spotted by a couple of cops. One of them becomes suspicious and on his own dime, follows up on the chance meeting. He hits paydirt when he learns of the stolen necklace then brings in girlfriend Delia (Martha Vickers) to seduce Nat into revealing where the necklace is. At the same time, the dirty cop (Stuart Bradley) goes to work on Gladden whom Nat has sent away for her protection against his partners, one of whom has already assaulted her. Turns out that Gladden is Nat's ward. Or maybe his foster sister after he'd been adopted by her father when he was a boy. Although Gladden is secretly in love with Nat, he's too hung up with the responsibility of taking care of her as he'd promised to her father to reciprocate. The resulting character interaction is interesting and quite a change of pace for the usually sleazy Duryea. Direction by Paul Wendikos is solid. Baby faced Mansfield and easy to fall for Vickers are good eye candy.

Everybody wants a piece of baby faced Jayne Mansfield in *The Burglar*, including Nat Harbin's henchmen. Here, she fends off the unwanted attentions of a member of her own gang

Whom Nat does manage to notice (and who wouldn't?) is Martha Vickers as the scheming Delia

Delia (Martha Vickers) gets the drop on Nat Harbin (Dan Duryea

Interesting POV shot from director Paul Wendikos as Dan Harbin (Dan Duryea) commits the robbery that sets in motion the events of The Burglar

The Brothers Rico (1957)

Eddie Rico is the mild mannered owner of a laundry business trying to make it away from the mob he used to work for as an accountant. But he soon learns that though it's easy to join the mob, it's a lot harder to break away. Out of the blue, his younger brother Gino appears seeking his help to disappear. Seems he was the hit man in a gang shooting and brother Johnny was the driver. Believing that the mob is out to get him to keep him quiet, Gino asks Rico to help him skip the country and go on the lam. Worse, a second brother, Johnny (James Darin) drove the gettaway car in the botched hit and has disappeared. Meeting with mob boss Sid Kubik (Larry Gates), Eddie is assured that the syndicate only wants his brothers out of the country. Nevertheless, they're concerned that the girl Johnny has married is related to a prosecutor who might persuade Johnny to turn states' evidence. Can he find Johnny and get him out of the country? Eddie agrees but it's all a set up...naturally! The mob has no intention of letting either Gino or Johnny get away.

Eddie Rico (Richard Conte) struggles whether to help his brother escape the vengeance of the mob knowing that to do so will drag him back into a world he tried to escape

Eddie Rico gets even

Eddie meets with the smooth talking mob boss Sid Kubik (Larry Gates) who assures him that he only wants to find brother Johnny to help him skip the country...

Dianne Foster provided the eye candy as Alice Rico

Eddie discovers that Kubik intended to betray him all along as local torpedos arrive to take out Johnny

The Sweet Smell of Success (1957)

Sidney Falco (played by Tony Curtis) is an unscrupulous small time agent who's only worth is his ability to get his clients mentioned in an influential column written by Walter Winchell wannabe J.J. Hunsecker (Burt Lancaster). In order to get those crumbs falling from Hunsecker's table, Falco becomes his willing creature running errands for him and doing his dirty deeds like trying to discredit up and coming musician Steve Dallas (Martin Milner) who's fallen in love with Hunsecker's sheltered sister Susan (Susan Harrison). There's a sub-text dealing with corrupt influence peddlers in the media lying just below the surface of the film, but it's most obvious subject deals with Hunsecker's unhealthy attachment to Susan for whom he'd do anything to keep from losing. Including having Franco frame Steve for possession of marijuana giving a dirty cop who owes Hunsecker a favor an excuse to rough him up. Despite a momentary twinge of conscience about the frame, Falco gives in when Hunsecker dangles the possibility of letting him write his column himself while the columnist goes on vacation with Susan. Alexander Mackendrick's direction of a script by Clifford Odets and Ernest Lehman is fast paced and in your face while location shooting on the streets of New York establishes a realism and immediacy to the action as characters exit restaurants and hotels onto traffic crowded thoroughfares in the city that never sleeps. Even with all outdoor scenes taking place at night, from the opening shots of newspaper delivery trucks roaming Time Square to storefront lunch counters, James Wong Howe's cinematography never falters, perfectly capturing the cold, pitiless feel of a New York City where everyone is on the make. Performances by both Lancaster and Curtis are the standouts though with Curtis just oozing sleaze and smarminess. For J.J. Hunsecker, Mackendrick chose to shoot Lancaster from low angles with overhead lighting that accentuated his menace. He described him as a "scholarly brute" and that's exactly the effect he got. With a weird stare through dark rimmed glasses, Lancaster projects a menacing self-righteousness that makes the viewer believe in his power to make careers or destroy people's lives, including his sister's. No set of superlatives can do justice to this picture. Just see it!

An adoring Sidney Falco (Tony Curtis) looks on as J.J. Hunsecker (Burt Lancaster) destroys someone's career over the phone

Shiny, brassy, busy New York City as lit by cinematographer James Wong Howe was a character in itself in *The Sweet Small of Success*

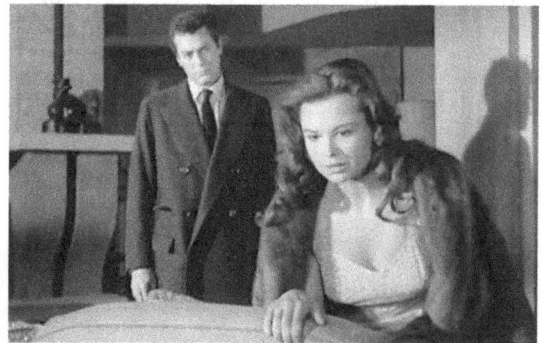

Susan Hunsecker (Susan Harrison) was the object of Steve Dallas' eye but also, fatally, that of her brother's as well!

The Lineup (1958)

Police procedural actually based on a radio and then TV show at the time. In it, psychopath Dancer (Eli Wallach) and friend Julian (Robert Keith) are hired to collect heroin that has been smuggled into the country by unknowing mules arriving from China. But right from the start, things go wrong as a local drug addict, hired to make the first pickup, loses control of the stolen cab he's driving, kills a policeman and dies himself in the crash. That sets the police on the trail of the racket going from clue to clue (and murder to murder left in the wake of Dancer and Julian's collection efforts). Eventually, Dancer and Julian collect all the smuggled heroin being forced along the way to killing some of the dupes involved. But their collection efforts hit a snag when they meet the last mules, a mother/daughter combination. Seems the daughter found the stuff inside her new doll and used it as face powder. Dancer is set to kill them outright but Julian talks him out of it explaining that the mother/daughter will be needed to explain to their employers that it wasn't their fault that part of the shipment was missing. Taking the pair with them to the drop, Dancer confronts their contact (known to him only as "the man") who refuses to accept his explanations and tells him that he's dead. Enraged, Dancer finally loses his cool and shoves the wheelchair bound crook over a balcony to his death on an ice skating rink. But by then the cops have zeroed in on them and a car chase follows that involves a tour of San Francisco until it ends on the unfinished Embarcadero Freeway. Fast moving film directed by Don Siegel and regular noir contributor Sterling Siliphant (who was all over noir in these years until he landed on TV's *Route 66*) is tight and lit as brightly by Hal Mohr as the sun splashed streets of San Francisco where exteriors were shot. Wallach is good as the barely under control Dancer and Keith as his keeper Julian (who likes to collect the last words uttered by Dancer's victims...until, in an ironic twist, Dancer shoots him and asks for his own last words as he lays dying). Richard Jaeckel is the pair's befuddled driver and look quick for a cameo by a young Michael Landon. This one's a keeper!

Location, location, location! A long shot from the climactic moments of *The Lineup* as Dancer and Julian's getaway car reaches the end of its road, literally, on the unfinished Embarcadero Freeway

200

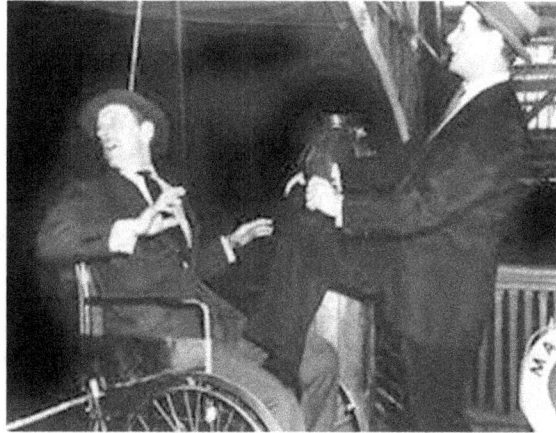

"You're dead!" An enraged Dancer (Eli Wallach) shoves "the man" over the balcony onto an ice skating rink below

Dancer (Eli Wallach), handler Julian (Robert Keith), and driver (Richard Jaeckel) take hostages Dorothy Bradshaw (Mary LaRoche) and her daughter Cindy (Cheryl Callaway) on a wild ride that ends on the unfinished Embarcadero Freeway

Murder by Contract (1958)

Claude (played by a very cool Vince Edwards) wants a change of career in order to make big money fast. To do it, he becomes a contract killer for the mob and right off, the film (with a tight, inventive script by Ben Simcoe and atmospheric direction by Irving Lerner) lets the viewer know that this isn't going to be a typical hired gun story. Making contact with mob boss Mr. Moon, Claude is forced to cool his heels in his hotel room killing time and waiting for the phone to ring. Finally, it does, and he has his first job. In a wordless montage, the viewer is treated to a number of Claude's early hits until he's ordered to take out Mr. Moon himself! Scene shift to Los Angeles where Claude is met by a pair of handlers, one who admires his cool professionalism and one who's impatient with his insistence on sight seeing until the very last minute. When that minute comes, Claude is upset to find that his target is a woman being held in protective custody. Suddenly, he loses his confidence saying women are unpredictable and so harder to plan around. This proves true when an attempt involving electrocution fails. Next, Claude uses diversionary tactics and shoots the woman when she comes to her door. Unfortunately, the woman he killed was a policewoman, something he learns only later. After Claude threatens to cancel the contract, his employers order his two watchdogs to kill him. They fail when Claude turns the tables on them. Now desperate to fulfill his contract and satisfy his employer, Claude makes his way into the house but just as he's about to strangle the woman, the police arrive forcing him to leave. Throughout, Lerner's pacing is perfect as suspense mounts first when Claude takes his time getting to work and later as his repeated attempts at killing the woman fail. In the meantime, his two watchdogs provide some black humor while Claude himself takes time to explain to them his cold blooded philosophy of life. Adding to the whole off kilter feel of the film is the hypnotic soundtrack by Perry Botkin which gives the feeling that the murderous goings on are not being taken seriously by the protagonists and might even be considered a lark by the unperturbed Claude. But the star of *Murder by Contract* is incontestably Edwards who radiates cool even when his character shows his psychological cracks: his distrust of women and a phobia regarding lipstick. Location work in Los Angeles is icing on the cake as Claude is conducted around town seeing the sights and taking a dip in the ocean. A must see!

Claude (Vince Edwards) moves in for the kill

202

Claude (Vince Edwards) explains his latest assassination plot to his impatient handler

It was only to be regretted that the very cool Vince Edwards didn't star in more films. Instead, he moved on to television starring in the popular *Ben Casey* series

City of Fear (1959)

City of Fear opens not with a prison break but after the break as Vince Ryker (Vince Edwards) escapes with a pal via police ambulance. As the film opens, we learn that his pal has been shot and Vince is in possession of a canister he thinks contains heroin worth a fortune on the open market but is really deadly cobalt-60. So deadly, that it's radiation is slowly killing Vince even through its lead casing. But if he ever opens it, everyone in Los Angeles, where he finally ends up, could be killed as well. Thus, the movie becomes a partial police procedural as the authorities try to track down and capture Vince before they're forced to inform the public and possibly start a panic. Meanwhile, Vince stops a hapless motorist and kills him. He leaves the man's body and that of his now dead pal in the burning hulk of the ambulance. Taking over the motorist's identity, he makes his way past roadblocks into the city where he first has a steamy encounter with girlfriend June Marlowe (Patricia Blair) and then makes contact with an ex-partner in crime who fronts as the owner of a shoe store. But things begin to go south for Vince as he grows sicker and the police catch up to him. Director Irving Lerner does a good job at the helm of this low budget item using clever camera tricks to liven things up. For instance, an interesting sequence takes place when a desperate Vince loses the canister and Lerner uses a subjective point of view to illustrate Vince's search of the interior of his car, whipping the camera about simulating his head movements. Of special note is the soundtrack by Jerry Goldsmith that makes even the dullest scenes exciting. Seamier L.A. locations add versimilitude to the action that cinematographer Lucian Ballard only puts the exclamation mark to. And as always, Edwards is magnetic in the lead as he goes from self-confident con to sick and desperate fugitive. His scenes with Blair in his motel room are convincing enough to make viewers believe that June would hold out against police grilling as long as she did. Although *City of Fear* echoes the earlier *Panic in the Streets*, it is its own film and much deserving of any fan's searching out.

Vince Ryker (Vince Edwards) makes contact with his shoe store fence in an attempt to sell what he thinks is a lode of heroin but is in reality, radioactive material

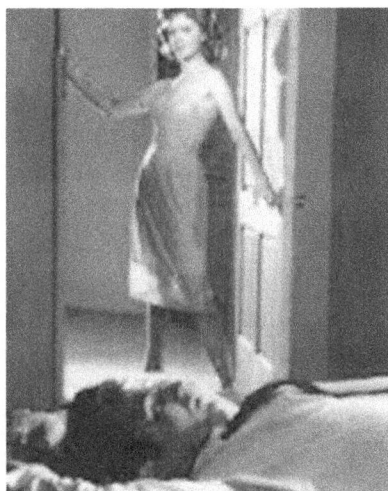

Patricia Blair as June Marlowe was more than equal to the task of keeping Vince Edward's Vince Ryker's attention!

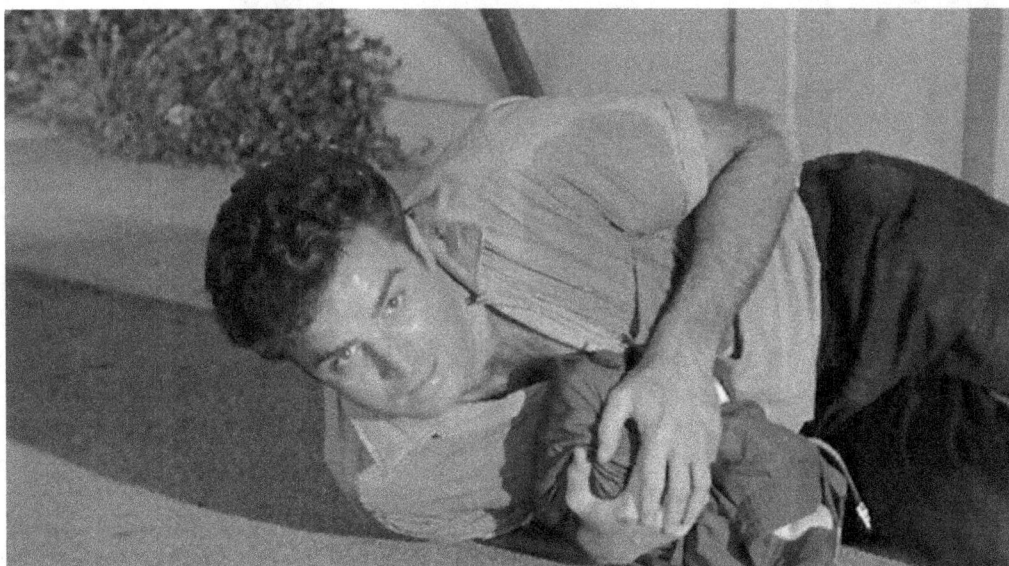

On his last legs, Vince Ryker desperately holds on to his deadly prize until the end

Sorry Wrong Number (1948)

Engrossing noir and told in series of flashbacks (sometimes flashbacks within flashbacks) that director Anatole Litvak never lets become confusing. Just the opposite! Things only get more and more intriguing as invalid Leona Stevenson (Barbara Stanwyck) first overhears a murder plot being discussed over the phone and then pieces together a mystery from a series of phone calls. A mystery that involves her father's pharmaceuticals company, gangsters, a police investigation, her husband's former girlfriend, and her husband Henry himself (Burt Lancaster). Nice cinematography by Sol Polito, especially in scenes on Staten Island beach as mysterious characters meet at a set of deserted buildings. Stanwyck is good as wife driven to near hysterics and Lancaster (by just donning a pair of glasses!) is convincing as a kept husband desperate to break loose from his wife's control. Litvak's direction is also daring at times with a number of pans around Leona's bedroom, circling the entire room or tracking through different rooms and even going downstairs. Fun supporting cast includes Wendell Corey as the doctor who diagnoses Leona as psychosomatic; Ann Richards as Henry's former squeeze; and Leif Erickson and Billy Hunt (who'd be reunited a few years later again as father and son in the classic *Invaders From Mars*!) as police detective father and his son.

Leona Stevenson (Barbara Stanwyck) listens as she overhears a plot to murder someone...someone who turns out to be her!

Henry Stevenson (Burt Lancaster) tries to warn Leona that she wasn't imagining things!

Lighting by Sol Polito turned a beach scene along Staten Island into this moody set piece where Sally Lord follows husband Det. Fred Lord to a midnight assignation

The Prowler (1951)

Webb Garwood (Van Heflin) is a small time creep in a cop's uniform when he and his partner are summoned to the home of Susan Gilvray (Evelyn Keyes) to investigate a report of a peeping tom. But when Garwood sets eyes on Susan, his tumble from one desperate situation to another follows the classic noir pattern...to the bitter end! The film may not have had the cinematographic chops as other films in the genre but director Joseph Losey and script writer Dalton Trumbo make up for that in spades as Garwood first seduces the married Susan, the shoots and kills her husband that he claims he thought was a prowler. Susan believes him and after an investigation in which they both lie about knowing each other prior to the shooting, Garwood is cleared and marries Susan. Using insurance money granted after the death of Susan's husband, Garwood sets them up as owners of a prosperous motel. Now their living in marital bliss. But a wrench is thrown into the neat set up when Susan declares that she's pregnant. The catch is, she was made so well before their marriage and since her former husband had been infertile, Garwood would be implicated and thus proved to have lied at the inquest. What to do? Since the production code forbade any thought of an abortion, the couple decide to hide out in a ghost town and deliver the baby themselves. From there, things go south fast and suffice it to say, there's no happy ending for the deserving Garwood! Losey's direction is flawless, keeping the story moving from one wrong turn after another, keeping the dominoes falling until the inevitable climax. Heflin is great as the conniving Garwood and although Keyes isn't attractive enough to convince the viewer that Garwood could fall so hard for her, she manages to convey the various emotions she's called upon to display. All in all, a must see for all noir fans!

Officer Webb Garwood (Van Heflin) first sets eyes on Susan Gilvray (Evelyn Keyes) as he looks through the same window where she reports a peeping tom had been looking

Garwood checks the body of Susan's husband whom he's just shot. Was it an accident or deliberate?

While not a raging beauty at the time she did *The Prowler*, Evelyn Keyes still had what it took to hook creepy cop
Webb Garwood!

Detour (1945)

Early noir that nevertheless follows the classic pattern in which lovelorn piano player Al Roberts (Tom Neal) decides to follow his girlfriend to California. Unfortunately, he has no money so ends up hitchhiking. Bad move! He ends up catching a ride with a pill popping bookie named Haskell who falls asleep while Al is driving. It starts to rain and after Al pulls over to put the top up, Haskell falls out of the car, hits his head, and is killed. That's when our boy makes his next bad move. He decides the police will never believe that Haskell's death was an accident, so he takes his wallet and leaves in the car! His next bad move comes when he in turn picks up a female hitchhiker named Vera (Ann Savage) who recognizes the car as one belonging to a man who gave her a ride earlier and who got fresh. After Al stupidly tells her all, she blackmails him by threatening to go to the police if he doesn't do as she says. Trapped, he hands over all his money and then agrees to sell the car and to turn the money over to her. Forced to pose as Vera's husband, they take a dingy hotel room where she has her latest brainstorm: with the death of Haskell's father, Vera wants Al to pose as his son to get the inheritance. That's the last straw for the now totally pathetic Al who refuses. Vera grabs the phone and retreats to the bedroom, locking herself in. There, she proceeds to call the police, laughing and taunting Al the whole time. Desperate, Al grabs the phone cord where it comes out beneath the door and pulls, strangling Vera. Even in death, Vera has the last laugh! Shot as a flashback, the viewer first picks up Al in a roadside diner clearly at the end of his rope as he recalls the events of the film. It ends in the same place as a defeated Al awaits arrest by the police. One of the bleakest of film noir, *Detour* goes all out showing how low a man can get as Al becomes Vera's virtual slave on a path that plunges ever downward to final oblivion. Directed by Edward G. Ulmer with practically no budget at all and with an amazing 68 minute running time, the plot is an attention grabber right from the start as the viewer wonders how Al hit bottom in the opening teaser. To be sure, neither Neal nor Savage are the greatest actors, nor is their dialogue terribly sparkling, but their characterizations of the pathetic, trapped male and the female glorying in her power over him (teasing him with taunts about sending him to the gas chamber!) is spellbinding. For the true connoisseur of film noir!

Naive Al Roberts (Tom Neal) stupidly spills his guts to ruthless Vera (Ann Savage)

End of the line for Vera in this interesting shot by director Edward G. Ulmer

A defeated Al Roberts (Tom Neal) awaits arrest at the end of *Detour*

Cape Fear (1962)

Excellent late period film noir made at a time when cinema noir had all but disappeared from theaters and moved to television. A number of attempts had been made by major studios to produce noir-like films (such as the big budget *Black Widow*) that failed due to over production and worse yet, the use of color. So it comes as somewhat of a surprise to find this film, shot in black and white with beautiful photography by Sam Leavitt, that totally captures the spirit of the genre. In it, Sam Bowden (Gregory Peck) finds his life turned upside down when Max Cady (Robert Mitchum), a man who was jailed for eight years due to Bowden's trial testimony and now released, begins stalking him. When Cady threatens his family, Bowden tries to sic the law on him but to no avail. The cagy Cady has done his homework and knows all the legal ins and outs. Finally, after his sadistic battering of a local girl underscores Cady's sick nature, Bowden is driven to desperation and devises a trap for the stalker that involves using his own family as bait. Directed by J. Lee Thompson with a script by James Webb, the story unfolds quickly and never lets you go. The tension mounts accordingly with every attempt by Bowden to stop Cady even as Cady is allowed to come and go as he pleases including terrorizing Bowden's daughter as she seeks to escape him through a darkened school building and finally ending up being struck by a car. Adding to the overall atmosphere of dread is the score by Bernard Herrmann; perhaps intentional as Thompson set out deliberately to give the film a Hitchcockian air. Given his earlier role in *Night of the Hunter*, Mitchum is in his element here as the threatening, relentless Cady. His climactic attack on Peggy Bowden (Polly Bergen) on the houseboat is justly memorable due to its improvisation including the famous scene where he crushes an egg in his hand then spreading the yolk caressingly over Bergen's body. And of course, Peck exudes righteousness and manly courage. Bergen does a creditable job as his frightened wife (especially in the near rape scene), Martin Balsam as the understanding police chief with his hands tied, and Telly Savalas as the private detective hired by Bowden to keep tabs on Cady. Lori Martin, as Bowden's tween daughter is noteworthy but one wonders at Bowden's judgement in allowing her to wear such brief outfits when he knows a pervert like Cady is stalking the family! An excellent film and a fitting last hurrah for a fading genre.

Sam Leavitt's atmospheric cinematography is on full display here as Cady threatens Peggy Bowden (Polly Bergen) with rape after smearing her with egg yoke

To underscore the threat Peggy Bowden will later face with Cady, an earlier scene has Cady taking loose woman Diane Taylor (Barrie Chase) to his room and brutalizing her

After viewers were fully informed about Cady's sadistic nature via the scenes with Diane Taylor, his continued surveillance of the Bowden family including daughter Nancy at the marina, reinforced audience dread of coming events. As the 1950s gave way to the 1960s, censorship became less stringent and the dangers that had always been implied in film noir became more explicit. Ironically, as they did, they killed the spirit of noir and the genre came to an end

The Third Man (1949)

Not an Orson Welles production but it should've been! Wells is perfectly cast as "the third man" carrying the body of Harry Lime from the flat where he'd just been murdered...except there was no murder, it was an elaborate fake designed to take the heat off Lime as the authorities in occupied Vienna close in on his black market racket. The fall guy is innocent dupe and Lime's childhood friend Holly Martins (Joseph Cotton) who appears on the scene pursuing a job offer from Lime. He ends up involved in Lime's scheme while falling in love with his girlfriend, Anna (Alida Valli). When British Major Calloway (Trevor Martin) shows Martins the results of Lime's illicit activities (children dying due to use of Lime's tainted vaccines), he decides to throw in with the authorities. That leads to the film's most dramatic moment when Lime is finally revealed in a nighted doorway, his cherubic face and friendly cat curling about his feet belying his ruthless nature. The film's next most memorable scene comes the next day when Martins meets Lime at a carnival. As they ride the ferris wheel, Lime gives his "cuckoo clock speech" one of the most memorable in all film noir as he explains his rationale for evil. Both scenes were brilliantly lit by cinematographer Robert Krasker who continues his magic in Vienna's sewer system as military police hunt down Lime in the movie's climactic scenes. It's hard to keep from raving about the whole look of *The Third Man* that Krasker turns into a mouth watering tour de force, the *neus plus ultra* of noir sensabilities. Literally ever scene is pure eye candy! Add to that Anton Karas' distinctive score performed on a zither, and you've got pure gold. And though all performances are solid, it's Welles' that steals the show. And even though he only makes his appearance three quarters of the way through, his personality impresses itself in every scene. Director Carol Reed's judgment is flawless throughout with liberal use of actual Vienna locations. Screenplay by Graham Green is top notch for suspenseful buildup to Lime's reveal and with enough complexity to keep the viewer glued to the screen for fear of missing the smallest detail. Possibly the best film noir ever. **Fun Fact:** Did you know that Greene had originally wanted a happy ending in which Martins walks off with Anna as his consolation prize? (He never did get that job after all) It's true. But he was overruled by Reed and producer David O. Selznick both of whom preferred the ending as shot; the long, long final take as Anna spurns Martins and walks away from Lime's grave.

The long goodbye: the final shot in *The Third Man* as Holly Martins is left behind by Anna

On the ferris wheel, Harry Lime (Orson Welles) explains the facts of life to Holly Martins (Joseph Cotton)

Cornered: In the Vienna sewers, Harry Lime is caught in Robert Krasker's brilliant cinematographic lighting